DESIGN STUDIO
2021 VOLUME 3

Design Studio Vol. 3 Designs on History: The Architect as Physical Historian is printed on Fenner Colorset Storm and Revive Offset Recycled 120gsm paper, FSC® Recycled 100% post-consumer waste. Papers Carbon Balanced by the World Land Trust. Printed with eco-friendly high-quality vegetable-based inks by Pureprint Group, the world's first carbon neutral printer.

© RIBA Publishing, 2022

Published by RIBA Publishing, 66 Portland Place, London, W1B 1AD

ISBN: 9781859469729
ISSN: 2634-4653

British Library Cataloguing-in-Publication Data
A catalogue record for this book is available from the British Library.

Commissioning Editor: Alex White
Assistant Editors: Clare Holloway and Lizzy Silverton
Production: Sarah-Louise Deazley
Designed and typeset by Linda Byrne
Printed and bound by Pureprint Group Ltd
Cover image: GROUPWORK + Amin Taha, Clerkenwell Close, 2017. Façade with the spire of St James, Clerkenwell. Photograph, Timothy Soar.

www.ribapublishing.com

About the Editor **V**

Dedication **V**

Acknowledgements **V**

Editor's Introduction
Jonathan Hill **IX**

ARTICLES

Architects of Fact and Fiction
Elizabeth Dow and Jonathan Hill **1**

The Architectural History of
Civilisation and My Design
Terunobu Fujimori **20**

Amateurs, Detectives and
Acupuncturists
Perry Kulper **30**

Apartheid's Architects
Lesley Lokko **42**

Drawing Together
Níall McLaughlin and Yeoryia
Manolopoulou **55**

Learning from La Vedette:
Reconstructing Viollet-le-Duc's
Alpine Study in Lausanne
Aisling M. O'Carroll **62**

Soft Memory
Pezo von Ellrichshausen **73**

Between the Borders of Utopia:
Towards a Construction of Time
Arinjoy Sen **85**

Explore, Restore, Ignore:
Etymology and Continuity in Design
Amin Taha **90**

A Monument is a Verb:
Parallel Geographies,
Choreographies, Atmospheres and
Other Forms of Monument
Sumayya Vally **100**

Final Word
Jonathan Hill **112**
Contributors **114**
Recommended Reading **116**
Index **118**
Image Credits **121**

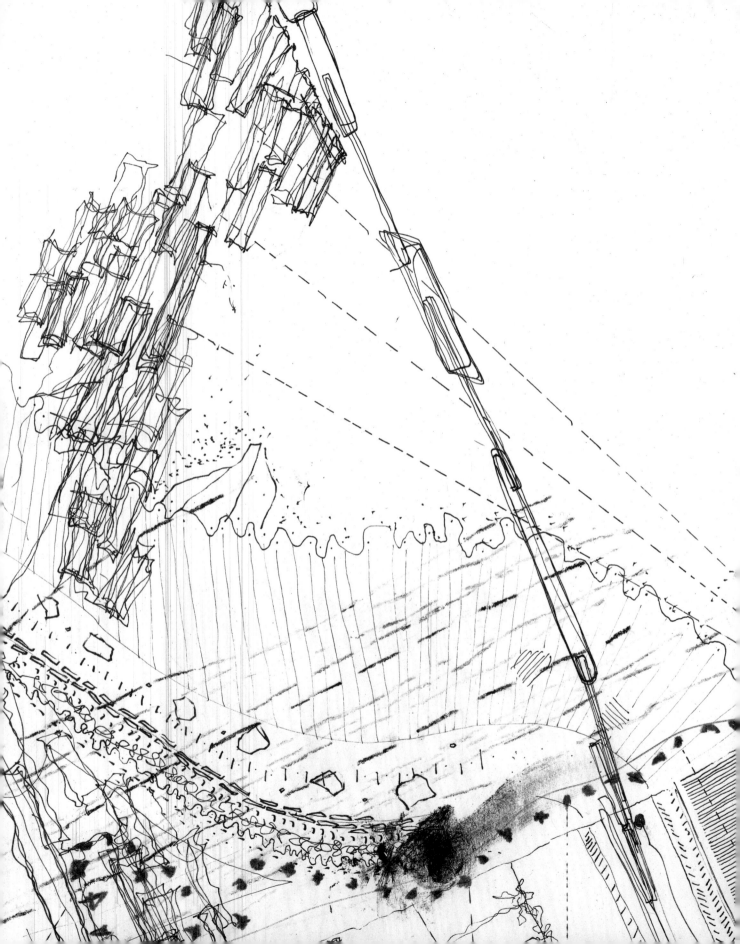

Designs on History

The Architect as Physical Historian

About the Editor

Jonathan Hill is Professor of Architecture and Visual Theory at The Bartlett School of Architecture, UCL, where he directs the MPhil/PhD Architectural Design programme and tutors MArch Unit 12. Jonathan is the author of *The Illegal Architect* (1998), *Actions of Architecture* (2003), *Immaterial Architecture* (2006), *Weather Architecture* (2012), *A Landscape of Architecture, History and Fiction* (2016) and *The Architecture of Ruins* (2019); editor of *Occupying Architecture* (1998) and *Architecture – the Subject is Matter* (2001); and co-editor of *Critical Architecture* (2007).

Dedication

To Dr Izabela Wieczorek, who inspires and encourages my research.

Acknowledgements

This book developed from my teaching and research at The Bartlett School of Architecture, UCL. I particularly wish to thank my teaching partners in MArch Unit 12, Elizabeth Dow and Matthew Butcher, for their stimulating and generous discussions, as well as my colleagues in the MPhil/PhD Architectural Design programme, especially Professor Ben Campkin, Professor Nat Chard, Professor Murray Fraser, Professor Penelope Haralambidou, Dr Jan Kattein, Professor CJ Lim, Professor Yeoryia Manolopoulou, Professor Sophia Psarra, Professor Peg Rawes, Dr Sophie Read, Professor Jane Rendell, Professor Bob Sheil and Dr Nina Vollenbröker. Also, at The Bartlett, I wish to thank Dr Eva Branscome, Barbara-Ann Campbell-Lange, Professor Edward Denison, Max Dewdney, Professor Adrian Forty, Chee-Kit Lai, Dr Guan Lee, Dr Luke Pearson, Professor Barbara Penner, Dr Tania Sengupta and Dr Tim Waterman. Dialogue with an exceptional group of MArch and PhD students has significantly influenced the character of this book, including Dr Alessandro Ayuso, Dr David Buck, Dr Inês Dantas Ribeiro Bernardes, Dr Felipe Lanuza Rilling, Ifigeneia Liangi, Aisling O'Carroll, Dr Natalia Romik, Wiltrud Simbürger, Dr Camila Sotomayor, Dr Quynh Vantu and Dan Wilkinson. I am also indebted to Ben Clement and Sebastian de la Cour; Professor Mark Dorrian, University of Edinburgh; Paul Fineberg; Catherine Harrington; Professor Toni Kauppila, Oslo National Academy of the Arts; Dr Amy Kulper, RISD; Dr Constance Lau, University of Westminster; Professor John Macarthur, University of Queensland; Professor Igor Marjanovic, Washington University, St Louis; Jean Oh; Franco Pisani; Rahesh Ram, University of Greenwich; and Neil Rawson. I value Ben Sykes-Thompson, Dr Jin Motohashi and Rei Sawaki for enabling my correspondence with Professor Terunobu Fujimori, and especially Rei for his generous and thoughtful translation. It is a pleasure to contribute to the exciting 'Design Studio' series and I appreciate the constructive support of Helen Castle, Alex White, Lizzy Silverton, Sarah-Louise Deazley, Linda Byrne and Clare Holloway at RIBA Publishing. Finally, I wish to thank all the contributors to *Designs on History*, who have made my experience as editor so stimulating and rewarding.

kelp

Orkney Drawing, 2018, 1:1 scale. *Drawing Together.*
Níall McLaughlin and Yeoryía Manolopoulou p 55

HUMAN FOSSILS

HOUSE 7

SEARA BRAE
HOUSE 1
DETAIL OF FIRE PLAN

DE I DISEGNI DELLE CASE DI VILLA DI ALCVNI
nobili Venetiani.   Cap. XIIII.

LA FABRICA, che ſegue è in Bagnolo luogo due miglia lontano da Lonigo Caſtello del Vicentino,& è de' Magnifici Signori Conti Vittore,Marco,e Daniele fratelli de' Piſani. Dall'vna,e l'altra parte del cortile ui ſono le ſtalle, le cantine, i granari,e ſimili altri luoghi per l'uſo della Villa. Le colonne de i portici ſono di ordine Dorico. La parte di mezo di queſta fabrica è per l'habitatione del Padrone: il pauimento delle prime ſtanze è alto da terra ſette piedi: ſotto ui ſono le cucine, & altri ſimili luoghi per la famiglia. La Sala è in uolto alta quanto larga,e la metà più: à queſta altezza giugne anco il uolto delle loggie: Le ſtanze ſono in ſolaro alte quanto larghe: le maggiori ſono lunghe un quadro e due terzi: le altre un quadro e mezo. Et è da auertirſi che non ſi ha hauuto molta conſideratione nel metter le ſcale minori in luogo,che habbiano lume viuo (come habbiamo ricordato nel primo libro) perche non hauendo eſſe à ſeruire, ſe non à i luoghi di ſotto, & à quelli di ſopra, i quali ſeruono per granari ouer mezati; ſi ha hauuto riſguardo principalmente ad accommodar bene l'ordine di mezo: il quale è per l'habitatione del Padrone,e de' foreſtieri: e le Scale,che à queſt'ordine portano; ſono poſte in luogo attiſſimo, come ſi uede ne i diſegni. E ciò ſarà detto ancho per auertenza del prudente lettore per tutte le altre fabriche ſeguenti di un'ordine ſolo: percioche in quelle,che ne hanno due belli,& ornati; ho curato che le Scale ſiano lucide,e poſte in luoghi commodi: e dico due;perche quello,che uà ſotto terra per le cantine, e ſimili uſi, e quello che và nella parte di ſopra,e ſerue per granari,e mezati non chiamo ordine principale, per non darſi all'habitatione de' Gentil'huomini.

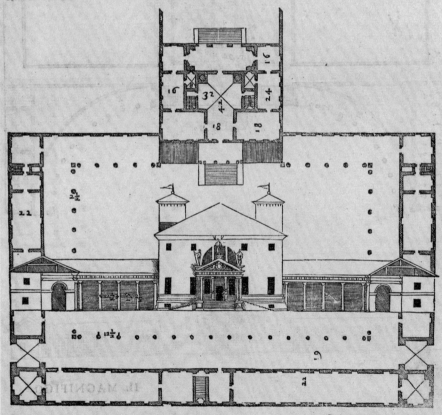

LA SEGVENTE

Editor's Introduction

Jonathan Hill

We expect a history to be written in words, but it can also be delineated in drawing, cast in concrete or seeded in soil. Conceiving the architect as a physical historian places architecture at the centre of cultural production, stimulating ideas, stories, values and emotions that inform and influence individuals and societies. To understand what is new, we need to consider the present, the past and also the future: we need to think historically.

The aims of this volume are to understand a design as a physical history, to investigate historical understanding as a stimulus to design and thus the ways in which architects learn from each other and other disciplines, and to consider the 'stories about history' that architects fabricate. The means to discuss these themes is the design studio, which is the basis of architectural education and practice. Academics and students concerned with practice and practitioners engaged with academia, the contributors have been selected because they exemplify the relevance of historical understanding to design and enable an international discussion. The contributors discuss the book's themes in relation to specific student projects, unbuilt designs and built works. Emphasising the creative interdependence of academia and practice, the design studio offers critical and constructive speculations on the state of architectural design, practice and discourse, stimulating the future development of the discipline.

Drawing the architect

The history of design is interdependent with the history of drawing. The term 'design' derives from the Italian *disegno*, which means drawing and associates drawing a line with drawing forth an idea. The Renaissance reasserted classical antiquity's appreciation of the timeless, immaterial geometries of ideal forms but introduced a fundamental change in perception to proclaim that drawing mediates seamlessly between the mind and the world, allowing the three visual arts – architecture, painting and sculpture – to be acknowledged as arts concerned with ideas. The command of drawing – not building – transformed the architect's status, establishing the influential myth that architecture results from individual, artistic creation not the combined knowledge of a construction team.

In contrast to the architectural drawing, which is seen in relation to other drawings and a building, the painting and sculpture are unique, thus appearing closer to the world of ideas. The architectural drawing depends on two related but distinct concepts. One indicates that drawing is an intellectual, artistic activity distant

Andrea Palladio, *I Quattro libri dell' architettura* ('The Four Books of Architecture'), 1570, bk. 2, p47. Villa Pisani, Bagnolo di Lonigo, 1569. Courtesy, RIBA Collections.

from the grubby materiality of construction. The other emphasises the architect's mastery of the collaborative building process. Creativity as well as confusion has arisen from this contradiction.

In 1563 CE the painter and architect Giorgio Vasari founded the first art academy, the *Accademia del Disegno* in Florence, which offered instruction in drawing and geometry, providing a model for art and architecture schools ever since. In the new division of labour, architects acquired complementary means to practise architecture: drawing, writing and building. To affirm their advanced status, they began to theorise architecture both for themselves and for their patrons, ensuring that the authored book became more valuable to architects than to painters and sculptors, whose artistic status was more secure and means to acquire and complete commissions less demanding.

Modelled on Vitruvius' *De architectura libri decem* ('Ten Books on Architecture') from the first century BCE, Leon Battista Alberti's *De re aedificatoria* ('On the Art of Building') was the first thorough investigation of the Renaissance architect as artist and intellectual, written in around 1450 and printed in 1485.[1] The first architectural book to be printed with illustrations, Francesco Colonna's *Hypnerotomachia Poliphili*, 1499, established the multimedia interdependence of text and image that has been essential ever since.[2] One model for the architectural book, *Hypnerotomachia Poliphili* is a fictional narrative illustrated with pictorial drawings. A second model is the analytical manifesto illustrated with orthogonal drawings, such as Andrea Palladio's *I Quattro libri dell'architettura* ('The Four Books of Architecture'), 1570. A further literary model, the manual conveys practical knowledge and is illustrated with diagrams. But these models are not hermetic, and many architectural books refer to more than one, as in Palladio's attention to practical matters.[3] The relationship between history and design was important to Colonna and Palladio. Historical references appear in both books but for different purposes. In one they enrich a specific story, in the other they legitimise generic solutions.

The Renaissance's concern for history was inseparable from its own history. Erwin Panofsky identifies a creative and critical nostalgia for classical antiquity 'that distinguishes the real Renaissance from all those pseudo- or proto-Renaissances that had taken place during the Middle Ages'.[4] In *Anachronic Renaissance*, 2010, Alexander Nagel and Christopher S. Wood write: 'The ability of the work of art to hold incompatible models in suspension without deciding is the key to art's anachronic quality, its ability really to "fetch" a past, create a past, perhaps even to fetch the future.'[5]

Often a design does not get built and an architect must be persuasive to see that it does. Sometimes building is not the best means to explore architecture. Influential architects tend to write, draw and publish, as well as build. Palladio is an early exponent of this tradition; Le Corbusier and Arata Isozaki are later exemplars. The relations between the drawing, text and building are multidirectional. For example, drawing may lead to building, writing may lead to drawing, or building may lead to writing and drawing. Listing the architectural works that inspire us, some would be drawings, some would be texts, and others would be buildings either visited or described in drawings and texts. An interdependent, multidirectional web of influences, drawing, writing and building have together stimulated architects' creative development for over 500 years.

A history of history

The earliest known histories originated over 4,000 years ago through record-keeping in Mesopotamia and Egypt, while the term 'history' derives from Ancient Greece. Between classical antiquity and the Renaissance, Western achievements in historical writing were no more significant than in the Islamic and Chinese worlds, and only in the fifteenth century CE did European historians begin to acquire the respect that their counterparts enjoyed in China.[6]

Neither Vitruvius' manuscript nor the earliest Chinese architectural treatise, which appeared in the technological encyclopaedia *Kao Gong Ji*, were conceived as histories. Describing actual events and others of his invention, Vasari's *Le vite de' più eccellenti pittori, scultori e architettori* ('The Lives of the Most Eminent Painters, Sculptors and Architects'), 1550, is the first significant history of Western art and architecture, initiating a new discipline.[7] In the sixteenth century, history's purpose was to offer useful lessons; accuracy was not necessary. In subsequent centuries, empiricism's emphasis on the distinction between fact and fiction transformed historical analysis. The historian began to employ a methodical, comparative method to characterise changing cultural, social, political and economic processes in which specific protagonists were contextualised. But this transition was slow and most eighteenth-century histories inherited some of the rhetorical approach of earlier histories, indicating that the truth does not depend on facts alone.

Factual fiction

The history of long prose fiction is around 2,000 years old, but the novel is a more recent innovation. The date and location of the first novel are disputed, depending on the literary tradition that is selected. Admired for its convincing depiction of court life in early eleventh-century Japan, Murasaki Shikibu's *Tale of Genji* is a candidate for the first novel. Other such tales veered closer to early historical writing and described real events. Often characterised as the first European novel, Miguel de Cervantes' *Don Quixote*, 1605–15, claims to be an accurate account of an actual person.[8] Michael McKeon assumes that the Catholic Counter Reformation ensured that Cervantes' sceptical, secular relativism was comparatively rare in seventeenth-century Spain.[9] The novel's development into a distinctive, popular literary form is often identified with early eighteenth-century England. In valuing direct experience, precise description and a sceptical, questioning approach to 'facts', empiricism created a fruitful climate for 'factual fiction'.[10] In contrast to the epic or romance, which incorporated classical myths and archetypes, the novel concentrated on everyday lives in enterprising, expansionist and increasingly secular societies, emphasising individualism as well as imperialism. The dilemmas of personal identity and fortune were ripe for narrative account. Frequently described as the first English novel, Daniel Defoe's *Robinson Crusoe*, 1719, is a fictional autobiography.[11] Defoe describes *Moll Flanders*, 1722, as 'a private History', and *Roxana*, 1724, as 'laid in Truth of Fact' and thus 'not a Story, but a History'.[12] The uncertain and evolving status of history supported authors' claims that their novels were histories. Even Jonathan Swift's *Gulliver's Travels*, 1726, is presented as true. A ship's surgeon and captain, Lemuel Gulliver claims to verify his story in a number of ways, including the donation of three gigantic wasp stingers to Gresham College, London, the first home of the Royal Society, the principal institution of British empirical science.[13] Swift mocks empiricism while employing its method.[14]

The early novels – fictional autobiographies – developed in parallel with early diaries – autobiographical fictions. People have written about themselves for millennia but the formation of modern identity is associated with a type of diary writing that Michel Foucault describes as a 'technology of the self', a process of self-examination by which moral behaviour is constructed.[15] Leading empiricists, such as John Locke and John Evelyn, maintained a diary as a means of personal development. Objectivity may be an aspiration, but no diary is entirely truthful, and the diarist cannot fail to reinvent life while reflecting upon it, altering the past and influencing the future. Equivalent to a visual, textual and spatial diary, the process of design – from one drawing to the next iteration and from one project to another – is itself an autobiographical 'technology of the self', formulating a design ethos for an individual or a studio.

In an era when information travelled slowly, the architect associated with *disegno* was just a century old in Britain when another appeared alongside it. In drawing greater attention to the conditions that inform self-understanding, the eighteenth century fundamentally transformed the visual arts' objects, authors and viewers, stimulating a new type of design and a new way of designing that emphasised the ideas and emotions evoked through experience. Ideas were understood as provisional, changeable and dependent on experience at conception, production and reception, rather than being universal. Landscapes not buildings were the initial design focus because they were more clearly subject to the changing natural world, which was associated with moral virtue and self-understanding.[16] The eighteenth-century estate was understood holistically in social, aesthetic, agricultural and ecological terms. The picturesque is a deceptive term because it emphasises one aspect of the eighteenth-century landscape to the detriment of its other qualities, such as the importance of the senses and the seasons to design, experience, understanding and the imagination. Rather than being conceived in a studio according to the rules of geometry, the picturesque was designed the way it was experienced, by a figure moving across a landscape and imagining multiple, alternative journeys, while special attention was given to drawings that explored the relations between site and experience. Stimulating fractured, self-reflective narratives and reimagining the past in classical reconstructions, antique sculptures and Mediterranean trees, the picturesque landscape is a novel and a history.

The multiple meanings of design

In the nineteenth century, an exponentially expanding market stimulated the subdivision of knowledge into specialisms in which the technocrat was the model practitioner. Associated with utility, the design disciplines that proliferated due to industrialisation were categorised as applied arts at best. Painters and sculptors discarded design once it became associated with collective authorship, mass production and problem

Giovanni Battista Piranesi,
Vedute di Roma, 1770.
Great Baths at Hadrian's
Villa, Tivoli. Courtesy,
RIBA Collections.

solving. Among the three original visual arts, only in architecture is the term regularly referred to today. In public discourse, design is more often associated with the newer design disciplines, but older and newer meanings are familiar in architectural discourse and practice. Whether they are academics or practitioners, architects combine multiple meanings of design because they reflect the histories and complexities of the architectural discipline.

Crude hints towards a history of my house

Mirroring the concern for the technocrat, history was increasingly equated to a science capable of objective statements, which led to an emphasis on archival research and formal analysis, establishing the art and architectural historian as an independent specialist distinct from art and design practice. However, historical and scientific statements are not neutral; each expresses a specific ideology. Just as much as any collection of papers, a building is an archive. But no artefact or archive can return the historian to the past and no analysis is more than an interpretation. Historical writing is diachronic, synchronic and anachronic.[17]

Despite the emergence of the specialist historian, the interdependence of design and history remained essential to the buildings and treatises of nineteenth-century architects. Rather than pseudoscientific, John Soane's appreciation of history refers to an earlier novelistic model, as in his *Crude Hints Towards a History of My House in L(incoln's) I(nn) Fields*, 1812.[18] Written while one house was demolished and a new one constructed, Soane imagines that his home is left to decay. Assumed to be haunted, the ruin has no visitors until a future antiquary attempts to decipher its earlier purpose and character. *Crude Hints* is a history of an alternative past as well as a history of a possible future, a genre with specific relevance to architecture given that a design is imagined before it is built and may take years to complete.

A society's historical, literary and artistic traditions shape its architectural stories. *Crude Hints* interweaves a novelist pretending to have rediscovered an authentic narrative and an architect employing archaeology to blur reconstruction and design, which Soane notably appreciated in the work of Giovanni Battista Piranesi. The Renaissance's allegiance to classical ideals ensured that the effects of time, nature and weather on buildings were deemed to be negative. But by the eighteenth century, the ruin's connotations were more complex and even positive, involving a temporal metaphor representing potential as well as loss, and an environmental model combining nature and culture. In 1815, in his tenth Professorial lecture at the Royal Academy of Arts, Soane states: 'And if artificial ruins of rocks and buildings are so cunningly contrived, so well-conceived, as to excite such reflections … they can be considered as histories open to all the world.'[19] Thus, a designed ruin is a history, and vice versa. Laying bare the processes of construction and decay while selectively discarding some material in favour of others, a history is a ruin of the past and a speculative reconstruction in the present. Emphasising the possibility for endless, alternative combinations and recombinations, a work of architecture, art or literature can remain unfinished, literally and in the imagination, focusing attention on the creative role of the user, viewer or reader as well as that of the architect, artist or writer.

Hybrid histories

Mirroring the expansion of worldwide trade and Britain's imperial reach, Soane's collection included objects from Egypt, China and South America as well as Europe. Emphasising Enlightenment reason, objectivity and progress, the Western idea of history spread around the world with the colonial powers. Rather than necessarily enlightening, it was a means to perpetuate Western ideology, establishing a benchmark against which alternative histories were deemed deficient.[20] Especially in the second half of the twentieth century, suspicion of metanarratives developed in many regions of the world, including the West. A historical method imbedded in scepticism became subject to scepticism. Although the Western idea of history remains influential and widely disseminated it has been informed and transformed by its travels. Other models are also evident. For example, there is a strong oral history tradition in Africa, where historical writing initially developed through contact with Christianity and especially Islam in North Africa.[21] History today offers not a singular model but a multiplicity of hybrid approaches, and concepts of fiction are equally varied, transforming architectural stories.

The history of the immediate future

Architects have used history to either indicate continuity with the past or departure from it. From the Renaissance to the early twentieth century, the architect was a historian in the sense that an architectural treatise combined design and history, and a building was expected to manifest the character of the time and knowingly refer to earlier eras. Modernism ruptured this system in principle if not always in practice. Walter Gropius excluded the history of architecture from the Bauhaus syllabus, advocating designs specific to the present and breaking from previous educational models. However, even early modernists who denied the relevance of the past relied on histories to validate and articulate modernism. Books such as Nikolaus Pevsner's *Pioneers of the Modern Movement*, 1936, and Sigfried Giedion's *Space, Time and Architecture*, 1941, identify a modernist prehistory to justify modernism's historical inevitability, rupture from the past and systematic evolution.[22] These authors present modernism as homogenous and primarily Western, implying that other regions should be judged against this model. For example, in China and Japan the idea of the architect as a designer, and architecture as an art, arrived with modernism. As a consequence, a premodern Japanese building could retrospectively become architecture and the architect could 'be interpolated, however anachronistically, between patron and master carpenter', writes Isozaki.[23]

In 1961 the Royal Institute of British Architects (RIBA) hosted two lectures in which the speakers, both historians, acknowledged mutual appreciation despite their disagreements, leading its President to quip: 'I hope we have not got to the stage when Pevsner speaks only to Banham and Banham speaks only to God.'[24] Responding to Pevsner's *Pioneers of the Modern Movement*, Reyner Banham's *Theory and Design in the First Machine Age*, 1960, proposes that the architect must 'run with technology'.[25] A year later Banham suggests a similar agenda for the historian in his RIBA lecture, 'The History of the Immediate Future'. Acknowledging 'the occupational risks of prophecy', he adopts a scientific analogy: 'History is to the future as the observed results of an experiment are to the plotted graph … History is our only guide to the future.'[26]

The architect as physical historian

By mid-century, modernism was no longer new, and was ripe for reassessment. Banham concluded that it was not yet modernist enough. But the Second World War was more scientific than the First, undermining confidence in technological progress as a means of social transformation. Notably for the generation of architects who saw military service, modernism's previously dismissive reaction to social norms and cultural memories became anachronistic. Modernism developed into a polycentric, worldwide network of distinct, varied and interdependent regional and local modernisms.

In 1966, a decade before Charles Jencks familiarised the term, Pevsner characterised the postwar designs of Le Corbusier and Denys Lasdun as 'postmodern', which he associated with the anxious aftermath of war: 'phases of so excessively high a pitch of stimulation can't last. We can't, in the long run, live our day-to-day lives in the midst of explosions'.[27] But it is more accurate to categorise their designs as simultaneously premodern, modern and postmodern. Associating history writing with storytelling, Lasdun remarked that each architect must devise their 'own creative myth', an evolving collection of ideas, values and techniques that spurs design, and concluded: 'My own myth … engages with history'.[28] In 1969, Vincent Scully stated that the architect will 'always be dealing with historical problems – with the past and, a function of the past, with the future. So, the architect should be regarded as a kind of physical historian … the architect builds visible history'.[29] Thus, the architect is a historian twice over: as a designer of buildings and an author of books.

As a design is equivalent to a history, we may expect the architect 'to have a certain quality of *subjectivity*' that is 'suited to the objectivity proper to history', as Paul Ricoeur concludes.[30] Historical writing requires imagination as well as analysis. However, the architect does not usually construct a history with the rigour expected of a contemporary historian and may combine qualities and genres instead.

Histories and novels need to be convincing in different ways. Although no history is unbiased, it must appear truthful to the past to have any validity. However, a novel may be believable but not true. In *The Fiction of Function*, 1987, Stanford Anderson emphasises that there was no coherent theorisation of functionalism in the early twentieth century and little indication that functionalism was rigorously applied to design. Instead, he argues: 'modern architecture, more than that of any other time, emphasized stories about function'.[31]

The architect is a 'physical novelist' as well as a 'physical historian'. Like a history, a design is a critical reinterpretation of the past in the present. Equally, a design is equivalent to a fiction, convincing users to suspend disbelief. We expect a history or a novel to be written in words, but they can also be delineated in drawing, cast in concrete or seeded in soil.

The times of design

While a prospect of the future is implicit in many histories and novels, it is explicit in many designs. Some architects conceive for the present, some imagine for a mythical past, while others design for a future time and place. Alternatively, an architect can envisage the past, present and future in a single architecture. Creative architects have often looked to the past to imagine the future, studying an earlier architecture to selectively appropriate and transform it for the present. In many eras, the most fruitful innovations have occurred when ideas and forms have migrated from one time and place to another by a translation process that is as inventive as the initial conception. A design can be specific to a time and place and a compound of other times and places.

Twenty-first century architects should appreciate the shock of the old as well as the shock of the new. To ask what is new involves other questions: why is it new, how is it new and where is it new? In William Gibson's memorable statement: 'The future is already here – it's just not very evenly distributed.'[32] To understand what is new, we need to consider the present, the past and the future: we need to think historically. Defining something as new is an inherently historical act because it requires awareness of what is old. A concern for innovation need not reject the past and sometimes the old is more radical than the new.[33] In many disciplines today, a number of practices and procedures of differing ages remain relevant and stimulating. The result is an interdependent network of diverse – new and old – models of architectural authorship that exist together, not simply because they are useful but because they also have social and cultural value.

Studying the history of practice as well as the history of architecture allows us to appreciate that architecture is not only made by architects. The contemporary relevance of interdisciplinary research, which occurs within, between and across disciplines, indicates that the profession is but one model of practice and implies that a combination of past and future models may be more rewarding.

The times of architecture

The value of historical understanding to design varies. Which issues are therefore of special significance today? The potential responses are numerous, and this volume's contributors answer in differing but overlapping ways to develop a fruitful and rewarding dialogue. My reply combines a concern for authorship, memory, time, geology and climate.

Design is familiarly understood as the first stage in a temporal sequence. But design, construction, maintenance and ruination can occur simultaneously while a building is in use, fluctuating according to

specific spaces and components. Accommodating partial ruination, focused repair and selective reuse can question the recurring cycles of production, obsolescence and waste that feed consumption in a capitalist society.

Architecture is made by use as well as by design and construction. Buildings and cities are most often experienced habitually when they are rarely the focus of attention. But habit is not passive. Instead, it is a questioning intelligence acquired over time and subject to continuing re-evaluation. Just as the reader makes a book anew, the user makes a building anew, whether through a physical transformation, a change of function or an unexpected association. But in contrast to the singular focused activity of a reader, a user performs, sometimes all at once, a series of complex activities, some habitual, others not, that move in and out of conscious attention.

Our perceptions and memories are fallible and creative. For example, the eyes receive inexact information and the brain extrapolates from previous knowledge and experience to create a plausible, seemingly comprehensive image.[34] Rather than just living in the moment, we filter the present through memories of the past and speculations on the future that are permeated by personal and collective values, weaving many times into one. As we move from place to place, we may seem to move backward or forward in time or oscillate between pasts, presents and futures.

Collective memory varies according to who is remembering and when. As some histories are forgotten and others reaffirmed, there is collective history as well as collective memory, which develop in dialogue with each other. In *The Seven Lamps of Architecture*, 1849, John Ruskin remarks that 'we cannot remember without' architecture[35]; yet each building is an attempt to forget some things and remember others.[36] Original meanings are soon obscured or transformed unless they are continuously reaffirmed through everyday behaviour and maintenance, which are as necessary to perpetuating collective memory as any material object.[37]

In previous centuries, knowledge of varied media pre-empted and informed physical experience, and vice versa. Contemporary digital technologies extend this condition to a more pervasive and persuasive degree. Today, we have many means to aid our recollections.[38] In each case to varying degrees, we transfer the mnemonic function from the person to the place. As it is not possible to literally carry a library of books or museum of artefacts, we still need to mentally edit what we have seen and experienced in these places. But personal communication devices store vast amounts

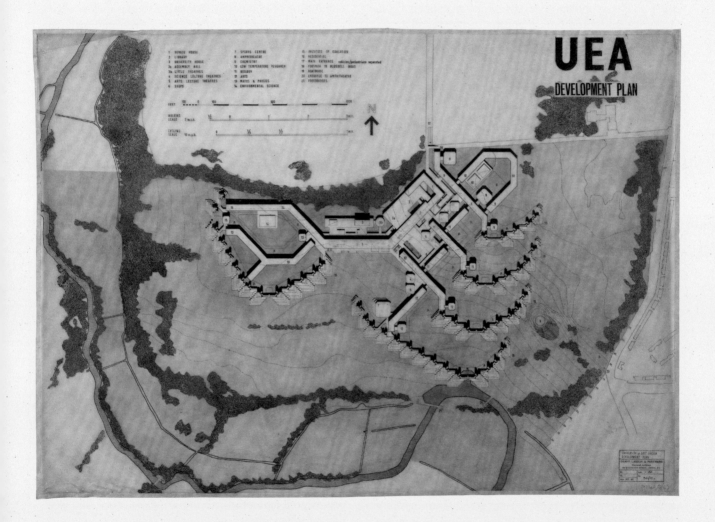

of information, changing the way that objects, images and events are viewed and remembered. The Internet enables speedy access to knowledge that was previously difficult to discover. Sharing the same information at the same time can facilitate local collective action, while on a regional or global scale it may encourage the interconnectedness of peoples and places. Equally, digital media can detach that information, and the people who view it, from an interdependent awareness of history, society and place. To a greater degree than before, personal communication devices undermine the need to recall and relate thoughts, forms and spaces in the integrated, immediate manner that is essential to a creative practice such as design. Historical thinking is evermore necessary in a twenty-first century society that needs to know how to remember and remember how to forget.

Architectural histories tend to adhere to a Western, linear conception of time but other histories are possible when time is understood as cyclical or non-progressive. Architecture changes, but it does not necessarily get better. We can learn from novels that freely move backward and forward in time and between types of time. We can also conceive alternative architectural histories if we acknowledge the timeframe of related disciplines, whether thousands of archaeological years or millions of geological ones. Assembled from materials of diverse ages from the newly formed to those centuries or millions of years old, and incorporating varied states of transformation and decay, a building is a time machine. Gazing at a marble wall, we can appreciate the geological 'Abyss' of deep time.[39] Our thoughts may be cast back to a prehuman era when ancient creatures inhabited the Earth or forward to a posthuman era when humans are extinct. If we contemplate a sedimentary stone, we see time's arrow and the possibility of ruin. If we gaze at an igneous or metamorphic stone, we see time's cycle and the possibility of repair.[40]

Linear, cyclical and non-progressive understandings of time co-exist in the seasons. The climate and weather have stimulated the architectural, artistic and literary imagination for centuries. John Evelyn's *Fumifugium: or The Inconveniencie of the Aer and Smoak of London Dissipated*, 1661, was the first book to consider the city's atmosphere as a whole and propose mitigation and adaptation as responses to anthropogenic climate change, three centuries before these principles were widely accepted.[41] Emphasising the allegorical, poetic and practical significance of his treatise, Evelyn

proposes that the edges of London are to be forested with trees and planted with fragrant shrubs so that wood could replace coal as the principal fuel and the whole city would be sweetly perfumed.[42]

Elected President of the Institute of Landscape Architects in 1951 – the first woman to head a UK design or environmental profession – Brenda Colvin appreciated Evelyn's advocacy of sustainable and regenerative development in the Royal Society's first official publication, *Sylva, or A Discourse of Forest-Trees and the Propagation of Timber*, 1664,[43] asserting that planting regimes were a responsibility inherited by the postwar Welfare State.[44] As the architect of the new University of East Anglia, Lasdun remarked that 'I became interested in designing buildings which responded almost ecologically to unique and specific situations' and recommended Colvin's appointment as the landscape architect in 1966.[45] Together they integrated landscape and architecture, appreciated the picturesque parkland setting, expanded the rich variety of natural habitats, and advocated a self-conserving system as far as possible. Despite the long history of environmentalism, and the burgeoning ecological movement in the 1960s, anthropogenic climate change was not widely acknowledged by scientists until the mid-1970s, leading present-day architects to sometimes forget the past and instead employ a debased technocratic empiricism devoid of the poetic and practical implications of Evelyn, Colvin and Lasdun's research.

Climate always changes, whether by anthropogenic or other means. Some critics of global warming imply that the current condition is an ideal that must be preserved, adopting moralistic religious metaphors in which environmental catastrophe is punishment for human failing, even though climate change is mostly incremental not sudden.[46] Ideas about climate express wider values, including attitudes to nature, ethics and governance. Science is also 'a cultural pursuit', as Mike Hulme emphasises.[47]

Studying the interconnected histories of architectural design and climate research enables us to better appreciate their conjoined future. The Hartwell climate researchers, including Hulme, Gwyn Prins and Steve Rayner, adopt the term 'wicked problem' to conclude that climate change is so complicated that it is beyond our ability to comprehend and solve.[48] First defined by Horst Rittel in 1967, who then published a paper with Melvin Webber in 1973, the term initially referred to planning not climate change, which suggests that architecture is also a 'wicked problem'. According to Rittel and Webber: 'Social problems are never solved. At best they are only re-solved—over and over again.'[49] In a similar vein, the authors of *The Hartwell Paper*, 2010, write that 'Rather than being a discrete problem to be solved, climate change is better understood as a persistent condition that must be coped with and can only be partially managed more – or less – well.'[50]

The dangers of global warming are real and need to be addressed when and where possible, notably because their effects are unequal, often causing greater harm to poorer, powerless communities. Awareness of climate change may also encourage cultural, social and environmental innovations and benefits, whether at a local, regional or global scale, including greater appreciation of the Earth and criticism of the isolationist policies of corporations and nations.

Among the Hartwell authors, the eighteenth-century gardener Lancelot 'Capability' Brown is a frequent reference, suggesting that an oblique approach may be effective in climate policy and landscape design: 'His advice would be to approach the object of emissions reduction via other goals, riding with other constituencies and gathering other benefits.'[51] The gardener and landscape designer are rewarding models for contemporary approaches to climate change, biodiversity and architecture because they acknowledge that we do not control nature and must work with, not against, it. At a casual glance, a landscape may appear to be subject to human order, and no more natural than another 'cultural' artefact. But despite the reduction of wildlife habitats and proliferation of pesticides, each landscape and building are teeming with creatures that are subject to their own rhythms and intertwined in a complex network of relations with other life forms, including humanity. Equally, we need to remember that people are natural as well as cultural beings.

Connecting the air to the earth, geology is a record of environmental and climate change. Geological time is ordered into distinct epochs defined by marked material transformations captured in geological strata. Naming or renaming a geological epoch is not just a question of science because it impacts on social, political and cultural priorities. Associated with glacial retreat over 11,700 years ago and the advent of human civilisations, the 'Holocene' was adopted by the International Geological Congress in 1885 and is still the established term for the current geological epoch. Etymologically it refers to two Ancient Greek words, *holos* and *kainos*, meaning 'whole' and 'new' respectively, and thus it is 'entirely new'. An alternative term, the 'Anthropocene',

came to public attention in 2000, when it was promoted by the Nobel Prize winning atmospheric chemist Paul Crutzen and the biologist Eugene Stoermer.[52] The beginning of the Anthropocene is disputed. In 2019, the Anthropocene Working Group (AWG) of the International Commission on Stratigraphy (ICS) – the largest division of the International Union of Geological Sciences (IUGS) – identified the mid-twentieth century as the start of the Anthropocene due to vastly increasing 'population growth, industrialization and globalization' allied to 'the artificial radionuclides spread worldwide by the thermonuclear bomb tests'.[53] The dominance of human civilisations is embedded within the terms 'Holocene' and 'Anthropocene', as well as an alternative, 'Capitalocene'. They are all anthropocentric. Dismissing 'technofixes' and fatalistic pessimism, Donna Haraway instead proposes the Chthulucene – from *khthôn*, meaning 'subterranean, of the underworld' – as the name for the geological epoch of a 'biodiverse', 'multispecies' and 'sympoietic' Earth.[54]

The unfinished Chthulucene must collect up the trash of the Anthropocene, the extremism of the Capitalocene, and chipping and shredding and layering like a mad gardener, make a much hotter compost pile for still possible pasts, presents and futures.[55]

Combining Brown's oblique approach with Haraway's 'mad gardener', an architecture that is analogous to an ever-changing landscape is more temporally aware than other buildings and will require constant re-evaluation, encouraging particularly questioning and creative relations between objects, spaces and occupants at varied times, scales and dimensions. The 'coproduction'[56] of multiple authors – human, non-human and atmospheric – is an appropriate model for architecture in an era of increasing geological, environmental and climate change. Consequently, the many cultural and natural protagonists involved in the life and death of a building all deserve the title 'physical historian'.

1 Vitruvius, *The Ten Books on Architecture*, trans. M. H. Morgan, New York, Dover, 1960; Leon Battista Alberti, *On the Art of Building in Ten Books*, trans. J. Rykwert, N. Leach and R. Tavernor. Cambridge MA and London, MIT Press, 1988.

2 Francesco Colonna, *Hypnerotomachia Poliphili: The Strife of Love in a Dream*, trans. J. Godwin, London, Thames & Hudson, 1999.

3 *The Four Books of Architecture* is the title of Isaac Ware's seminal English translation of 1738, but Palladio's treatise has also been translated as The Four Books on Architecture. Andrea Palladio, *The Four Books on Architecture*, trans. R. Tavernor and R. Schofield, Cambridge MA, MIT Press, 1997, bk 1, chs 1–10, pp 6–16; bk 2, chs 12–15, pp 45–68. For an alternative categorisation of architectural books, refer to Adrian Forty, 'Architectural Description: Fact or Fiction?' in *When Architects and Designers Write, Draw and Build?: Essays on Architecture and Design Research*, eds. J. Dehs, M. W. Esbensen and C. P. Pedersen, Aarhus, Arkitektskolens Forlag, 2013, pp 200–201.

4 Erwin Panofsky, '*Et in Arcadia Ego*: Poussin and the Elegiac Tradition' in *Meaning in the Visual Arts*, Chicago, University of Chicago Press, 1982, pp 302–333, first published in 1955.

5 Alexander Nagel and Christopher S. Wood, *Anachronic Renaissance*, New York, Zone Books, 2010, pp 13–18.

6 Daniel Woolf, *A Global History of History*, Cambridge, Cambridge University Press, 2011, pp 23, 34–35, 89, 172, 227.

7 Giorgio Vasari, *The Lives of the Most Excellent Painters, Sculptors, and Architects*, trans. G. C. de Vere, New York, Random House, 2006.

8 Miguel de Cervantes, *Don Quixote*, trans. J. Ormsby, https://www.gutenberg.org/files/996/996-h/996-h.htm, 1605–1615, (accessed 24 March 2020), 'Author's Preface'.

9 Michael McKeon, *The Origins of the English Novel 1600–1740*, Baltimore, The Johns Hopkins University Press, 1987, p 293.

10 Lennard J. Davis, *Factual Fictions: The Origins of the English Novel*, Philadelphia, University of Pennsylvania Press, 1996, p 213, first published in 1983. Refer to Edward Said, *Culture and Imperialism*, New York, Vintage Books, 1994, pp 70–80, first published in 1993.

11 Daniel Defoe, *Robinson Crusoe*, Oxford, Oxford University Press, 2007.

12 Daniel Defoe, *Moll Flanders*, New York, Norton, 2004, p 3; Daniel Defoe, *Roxana, or the Fortunate Mistress*, ed. P. N. Furbank, London, Pickering and Chatto, 2009, p 21.

13 The Society was founded in 1660 after Christopher Wren's inaugural lecture and received a royal charter two years later with the purpose to advance scientific knowledge through empirical investigation. Wren was Professor of Astronomy at Gresham College.

14 Jonathan Swift, *Gulliver's Travels*, https://www.gutenberg.org/files/829/829-h/829-h.htm, 1726, pt 2, ch 3 (accessed 24 March 2020).

15 Michel Foucault, 'On the Genealogy of Ethics: An Overview of Work in Progress' in *The Foucault Reader*, ed. P. Rabinow, London, Penguin, 1984, p 369; Michel Foucault, 'Technologies of the Self' in *Technologies of the Self: A Seminar with Michel Foucault*, eds. L. H. Martin, H. Gutman and P. H. Hutton, London, Tavistock, 1988, pp 18–19.

16 Anthony Ashley Cooper, third Earl of Shaftesbury, *Characteristicks of Men, Manners, Opinions, Times*, Oxford, Clarendon Press, 1999, vol 2, p 101, first published as a three-volume collection in 1711.

17 Sylviane Agacinski, *Time Passing: Modernity and Nostalgia*, New York, Columbia University Press, 2003, p 113.

18 John Soane, 'Crude Hints Towards an History of my House in L(incoln's) I(nn) Fields' in *Visions of Ruin: Architectural Fantasies and Designs for Garden Follies*, ed. C. Woodward, London, Sir John Soane's Museum, 1999, pp 61–75.

19 John Soane, 'Lecture X', in David Watkin, *Sir John Soane: Enlightenment Thought and the Royal Academy Lectures*, Cambridge, Cambridge University Press, 1996, p 626. Refer to Inger Sigrun Brodey, *Ruined by Design: Shaping Novels and Gardens in the Culture of Sensibility*, London and New York, Routledge, 2008, p 117.

20 Edward Said, *Orientalism*, London, Penguin, 2001, pp 31–110; John Tosh, *The Pursuit of History: Aims, Methods and New Directions in the Study of History*, London and New York, Routledge, 2015, sixth edition, pp 241–250.

21 Woolf, *A Global History of History*, pp 7, 440, 445.

22 *Pioneers of the Modern Movement* was reprinted as *Pioneers of Modern Design* in 1949 and revised in 1960. Nikolaus Pevsner, *Pioneers of the Modern Movement: From William Morris to Walter Gropius*, London, Faber & Faber, 1936; Sigfried Giedion, *Space, Time and Architecture: The Growth of a New Tradition*, Cambridge MA, Harvard University Press, 1967.

23 Arata Isozaki, 'Authorship of Katsura: The Diagonal Line', in *Japan-ness in Architecture*, trans. S. Kohso, ed. D. B. Stewart, Cambridge MA and London, MIT Press, 2006, p 293.

24 William Holford, in Nikolaus Pevsner, 'Modern Architecture and the Historian or The Return of Historicism', *Journal of the Royal Institute of British Architects*, vol 68, no 6, April 1961, p 239.

25 Reyner Banham, *Theory and Design in the First Machine Age*, London, The Architectural Press, 1960, pp 329–330.

26 Reyner Banham, 'The History of the Immediate Future', *Journal of the Royal Institute of British Architects*, vol 68, no 7, May 1961, p 252.

27 Nikolaus Pevsner, 'The Anti-Pioneers' in *Pevsner on Art and Architecture: The Radio Talks*, ed. S. Games, London, Methuen, 2002, pp 299, 307. For the earliest use of the term with regard to architecture, refer to Joseph Hudnut, 'The Post-Modern House', *Architectural Record*, no 97, May 1945, pp 70–75.

28 Denys Lasdun, 'The Architecture of Urban Landscape' in *Architecture in an Age of Scepticism: A Practitioner's Anthology Compiled by Denys Lasdun*, ed. D. Lasdun, London, Heinemann, 1984, pp 137, 139.

29 Vincent Scully, *American Architecture and Urbanism*, London, Thames & Hudson, 1969, p 257.

30 Paul Ricoeur, 'Objectivity and Subjectivity in History' in *History and Truth*, trans. C. A. Kelbley, Evanston, Northwestern University Press, 1965, p 22. Refer to Paul Ricoeur, *Time and Narrative, Volume 3*, trans. K. Blamey and D. Pellauer, Chicago and London, University of Chicago Press, 1988, pp 99, 243.

31 Stanford Anderson, 'The Fiction of Function', *Assemblage*, no. 2, February 1987, p 21.

32 William Gibson, https://quoteinvestigator.com/2012/01/24/future-has-arrived, (accessed 24 March 2020).

33 David Edgerton, *The Shock of the Old: Technology and Global History Since 1900*, London, Profile, 2008, p. 212.

34 Richard Gregory, *Eye and Brain: The Psychology of Seeing*, Oxford, Oxford University Press, 1998, pp 5, 10.

35 John Ruskin, *The Seven Lamps of Architecture*, New York, Farrar, Straus and Giroux, 1981, pp 169.

36 Adrian Forty, 'Introduction' in *The Art of Forgetting*, eds. A. Forty and S. Küchler, Oxford and New York, Berg, 1999, p 16.

37 Edward S. Casey, *Remembering: A Phenomenological Study*, Bloomington and Indianapolis, Indiana University Press, 2000, p xiii; Maurice Halbwachs, *The Collective Memory*, New York, Harper Colophon Books, 1980, pp 78–84, first published as *La Mémoire Collective*, 1950.

38 Casey, *Remembering*, p 2; Frances A. Yates, *The Art of Memory*, London and New York, Routledge, 1999, p 4.

39 Stephen Jay Gould, *Time's Arrow, Time's Cycle: Myth and Metaphor in the Discovery of Geological Time*, London, Penguin, 1990, p 61, first published in 1987.

40 Gould, *Time's Arrow, Time's Cycle*, p 65.

41 John Evelyn, *Fumifugium: Or, The Inconveniencie of the Aer, and Smoake of London Dissipated*, London, B. White, 1772, pp 3, 28, 34–37, first published with a slightly different title.

42 Evelyn, *Fumifugium*, pp 47–49. Refer to Mark Jenner, 'The Politics of London Air: John Evelyn's *Fumifugium* and the Restoration', *The Historical Journal*, vol 38, no 3, 1995, pp 544–446.

43 Identifying a more sensitive attitude to the modification of nature than before, Clarence J. Glacken mentions *Sylva* and the *French Forest Ordinance of 1669*, initiated by Jean-Baptiste Colbert, minister to Louis XIV. John Croumbie Brown, ed., *French Forest Ordinance of 1669*, Edinburgh, Oliver and Boyd and London, Simpkin, Marshall and Co., 1883; John Evelyn, *Sylva, or A Discourse of Forest-Trees, and the Propagation of Timber in His Majesties Dominions*, London, Royal Society, 1664, pp 112–120; Clarence J. Glacken, *Traces on the Rhodian Shore: Nature and Culture in Western Thought from Ancient Times to the End of the Eighteenth Century*, Berkeley, University of California Press, 1967, p 485.

44 Brenda Colvin, letter to Frank Thistlethwaite, Vice-Chancellor, University of East Anglia, 4 November 1968, Colvin & Moggridge Archive.

45 Lasdun, 'The Architecture of Urban Landscape', p 135.

46 Michel Crucifix and James Annan, 'Is the Concept of "Tipping Point" Helpful for Describing and Communicating Possible Futures?' in *Contemporary Climate Change Debates: A Student Primer*, ed. M. Hulme, London and New York, Routledge, 2020, pp 23–35.

47 Mike Hulme, *Weathered: Cultures of Climate*, London, Sage, 2017, p xiii.

48 Mike Hulme, *Why We Disagree About Climate Change*, Cambridge, Cambridge University Press, 2009, p 334; Gwyn Prins and Steve Rayner, *The Wrong Trousers: Radically Re-Thinking Climate Policy*, LSE and University of Oxford, http://eureka.sbs.ox.ac.uk/66/1/TheWrongTrousers.pdf, 2007, p v (accessed 3 February 2020); Gwyn Prins, Isabel Galiana, Christopher Green, Reiner Grundmann, Mike Hulme, Atte Korhola, Frank Laird, Ted Nordhaus, Roger Pielke Jr, Steve Rayner, Daniel Sarewitz, Michael Shellenberger, Nico Stehr and Hiroyuki Tezuka. *The Hartwell Paper: a new direction for climate policy after the crash of 2009*, LSE and University of Oxford, https://eprints.lse.ac.uk/27939/1/HartwellPaper_English_version.pdf, 2010, pp 15–16 (accessed 3 February 2020).

49 Horst W. J. Rittel and Melvin M. Webber, 'Dilemmas in a General Theory of Planning', *Policy and Sciences*, vol 4, no 2, June 1973, p 160.

50 Prins et al., *The Hartwell Paper*, p 16.

51 Prins and Rayner refer to Brown because he is better known but William Kent was the true innovator of the oblique approach, as at Rousham, 1737–41, and Stowe, 1730–48. Brown worked for Kent at Stowe and later succeeded him as head gardener. Prins and Rayner attribute the phrase 'Lose the object and draw nigh obliquely' to Brown and refer to William Shenstone, *Unconnected Thoughts on Gardening*, 1764. The reference to Capability Brown was first made by Steve Rayner and appears in Prins and Rayner, *The Wrong Trousers*, pp 38–39; Prins et al., *The Hartwell Paper*, p 9. Refer to Mike Hulme, *Can Science Fix Climate Change? A Case Against Climate Engineering*, Cambridge, Polity Press, 2014, p 115.

52 Paul J. Crutzen and Eugene F. Stoermer, 'The Anthropocene', *IGBP Global Change Newsletter*, no 41, May 2000, pp 17–18. Refer to Simon Lewis and Mark Maslin, 'Defining the Anthropocene', *Nature*, vol 519, no 7542, 12 March 2015, pp 172–173.

53 Anthropocene Working Group, *'What is the Anthropocene?—Current Definition and Status'*, Subcommission on Quarternary Stratigraphy and International Commission on Stratigraphy, 21 May 2019, http://quaternary.stratigraphy.org/working-groups/anthropocene (accessed 7 January 2021).

54 Donna J. Haraway, *Staying with the Trouble: Making Kin in the Chthulucene*, Durham NC and London, Duke University Press, 2016, pp 2–3, 55.

55 Haraway, p 57.

56 Steve Rayner refers to 'coproduction' and Jane Bennett refers to 'distributed agency', while Carolyn Merchant recognises a 'partnership' in which 'both humans and nature are active' and nature is not gendered. Herbert Marcuse conceives nature as active, sometimes humanity's 'ally', sometimes hostile. Steve Rayner 'Domesticating Nature: Commentary on the Anthropological Study of Weather and Climate Discourse' in *Weather, Climate, Culture*, eds. S. Strauss and B. Orlove, Oxford and New York, Berg, 2003, p 287; Jane Bennett, *Vibrant Matter: A Political Ecology of Things*, Durham NC and London, Duke University Press, 2010, p 38; Carolyn Merchant, *Reinventing Eden: The Fate of Nature in Western Culture*, New York and London, Routledge, 2003, pp 223–231; Herbert Marcuse, *Counterrevolution and Revolt*, Boston, Beacon Press, 1972, pp 65, 69.

Tom Noonan, *John Evelyn Institute of Arboreal Science*, 2010. River panorama.

Architects of Fact and Fiction

**Elizabeth Dow
and Jonathan Hill**

As dialogical tutors, our aim is to create a coherent position that is also questioning and incomplete, and thus a stimulus to each person's creative development, facilitating a generous design community of individuals. We encourage each student to develop their 'own creative myth',[1] an evolving collection of ideas, values and techniques that spurs design, and to foster friendships and associations that will sustain future careers.

At the start of the academic year, we galvanise Unit 12 students at The Bartlett School of Architecture, UCL, to trust intuition as a form of intelligence based on knowledge and experience, identifying a catalyst to the imagination that can then develop in conjunction with critical reflection. A creative dialogue should also exist between design intention and working medium. Often, the most fruitful innovations develop between distinct but related media, such as analogue and digital drawing, encouraging the designer to conceptualise their place within this process. Design is a form of critical and creative play, tricking and surprising us to understand and question presumptions and prejudices.

Our concern is the relevance of the past – recent or distant – to the present and future, speculating on the question: how and why might this happen now? As well as history, we are interested in personal history. When everybody else is looking at one time and place, it's always good to look elsewhere as a discovery may be yours alone, and thus more surprising for everyone. Exceptional architects are exceptional storytellers. Such tales have special significance when they resonate back-and-forth between private inspiration and public narrative.

Architecture is about bricks and mortar and concrete does follow formwork, but these seemingly quite pragmatic statements can and often do mask the complex set of research questions that each student and architect must ask themselves to determine the when, why, how, from what and for whom a building might be constructed. Whilst we see speculation and an ability to conflate fact and fiction as a vital part of our approach to the study of architecture,[2] this does not mean that Unit 12 students do not have equal determination and genuine passion to understand how architecture is built, from inception to completion, appreciating the joy of the small detail that informs the big picture. To suggest that architectural practice is the 'real world', and education is somehow less real, misses the point. It fails to recognise that building the skills of speculation, the ability to ask 'what if?', and the rigour of constructing a research-based position, allow each student, and subsequently each architect, to be much more able to hold their ground and convince others.

To create architecture you need imagination, passion, empathy, originality, a knowing respect for the past and a positive anticipation of the future. You need to be able to tell a story and to solve problems, you need to be able to convince others of your ideas but also to listen. An original idea is very rare, but to posit an original approach that builds upon existing research and experience is an invaluable skill.

Architecture does not exist in a vacuum; it has always been informed by multiple disciplines – history, politics, art, craft, philosophy, gardening – and communicated through a range of media that complement and even validate each other. Students must understand that it is not merely the skills within these disciplines that should be appropriated, but also the ability to look at a question and then answer it from a number of perspectives. By allowing the resulting architecture to encompass the bigger picture one can more easily enter into and contribute to contemporary debates such as sustainability and climate change. To bring the nuanced knowledge of other observations, languages and means of communication to the production of architecture broadens the debate beyond the short term and obvious – the regulatory and reactionary – to see change as positive, as welcoming as it is inevitable, and as life-affirming.

Acknowledging that differing conceptions of change exist in conjunction today, Unit 12 understands a monument and a ruin as creative, interdependent themes within a single building, which may fall into decay, rise into built form or oscillate between the two, further intensifying the already blurred relations between the constructed, ruined and unfinished. As its etymology derives from *monere*, meaning to remind, warn and advise, the monument's purpose is complex and questioning and not merely commemorative, while the ruin is a temporal metaphor representing potential as well as loss and an environmental model combining nature and culture.

The inevitability of change – whether of climate, ethics, governance or use – requires us to consider the future as well as the present, notably as a design may take years to complete. How should a building react when, for example, it is predicted that London will have the climate of Barcelona or Melbourne by 2050?[3] How long should a building last? 100 years? 1,000 years?

In response to anthropogenic climate change and in support of sustainable and regenerative development, we propose that buildings should be designed to endure and adapt, emphasising longevity not obsolescence. Conceiving construction, maintenance and ruination as simultaneous and ongoing processes, our designs are drawn in varied times and states. Appreciating the interaction of public and private lives, we emphasise that architecture is political, and use is transformative.

Acknowledging the creative influence of multiple authors – human, non-human and atmospheric – the following projects developed in Unit 12 conceive architectures that work in symbiotic interdependence with the hybrid conditions of their immediate and wider environments. Sometimes competing, sometimes affirming, each author may inform the other, as in a feisty dialogue of distinct voices and unexpected conclusions in which authorship is temporal and shared.

John Evelyn Institute of Arboreal Science (previous page)
Advocating the poetic and practical implications of Evelyn's seventeenth-century environmental research as a model for contemporary architecture and landscape, the *John Evelyn Institute of Arboreal Science* is built close to the site of his demolished house in east London, where the royal dockyard was once located.[4] The new dock is an ever-changing stage animated by the Institute's activities, developing renewable energy systems and sustainable building practices. Extensive reforestation of the Thames Estuary reduces global warming and reinvigorates the timber construction industry. London is rebuilt in a renewable building material and the Thames is once again a working river. Combining old and new technologies, Tom Noonan's hybridisation of analogue and digital drawing techniques encapsulates the Institute's ethos.

London City Farmhouse

Asking how far we should take recycling and reuse, the *London City Farmhouse* is a riverside prototype for a self-sufficient community that integrates agriculture, housing and vertical public gardens. Noting that advocates of sustainability sometimes adopt moralistic religious metaphors in which environmental catastrophe is the punishment for human failing, space is the reward for those who contribute and a diminished lifestyle is the outcome for others who do not cooperate. Colour theory informs the choice of materials with specific hues selected for their laxative properties; all types of waste are potential energy sources.

Catrina Stewart, *London City Farmhouse*, 2011. River elevation.

FX Beauties Club

An association of Japanese housewives, the FX Beauties, challenges stereotypes of gendered domesticity through successful careers as currency speculators. Designed, explored and expressed through a large-scale model of lacquered, polished, veneered and mirrored materials, the *FX Beauties Club* sits in critical dialogue with the male-only clubs of London's Pall Mall, and in stark contrast to the solid Portland stone of the adjacent Reform Club.

**Christine Bjerke,
FX Beauties Club,
2013. Exterior.**

Left: Ifigeneia Liangi,
*A Primary School for
Athens,* 2012. The lovers'
tree house.

Right: Ifigeneia Liangi,
*A Primary School for
Athens,* 2012. The giant.

A Primary School for Athens

Ifigeneia Liangi characterises the contemporary Greek crisis as an economic,
political and social catastrophe rooted in the nation's recent history. Located
in central Athens, the primary school's purpose is to re-educate a nation in
civic responsibility and thus re-envision democracy. Critically transformed
for their new scale and setting, buildings and spaces mimic the principal
state institutions, allowing children to play out scenes, operate their own
parliaments, courts and libraries and learn how to address the inequities
of their parents' and grandparents' generations. Drawing on fairy tales and
collective memories, the magic realist architecture is playful, scenographic
and at times sinister, offering a socio-political, poetic and allegorical critique
of the present, and suggesting possible but improbable futures.

The Living Dam

In response to the UK's water shortage and inadequate hydrological infrastructure, Louis Sullivan conceives a new typology for a reservoir that incorporates a small town in the curved, outer slope of a dam. Sequential terraces incorporate housing and public facilities among ponds, reedbeds, watercress fields and fruit gardens, which are maintained by the inhabitants to develop the symbiotic interdependence of town and reservoir, generating pure water, productive ecologies and communal responsibility.

Louis Sullivan, *The Living Dam*, 2014. Sectional perspective.

Benjamin Ferns, *Pontifical Academy of Sciences*, 2015. Apostolic library.

Designs on History: The Architect as Physical Historian

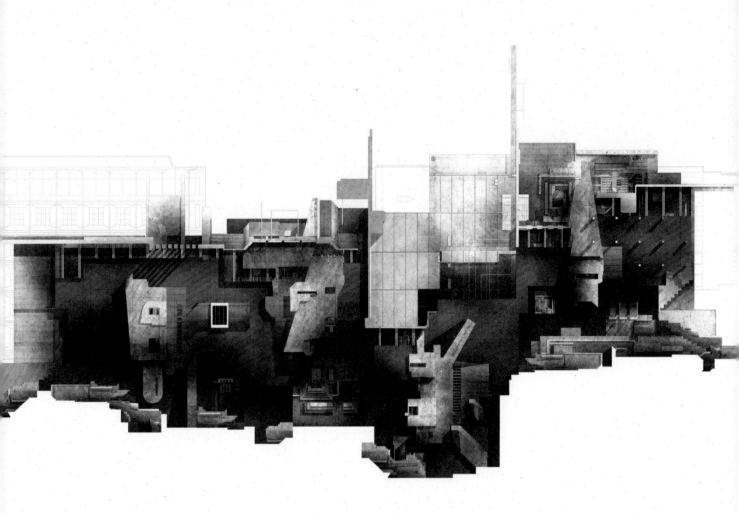

Pontifical Academy of Sciences

The *Pontifical Academy* has its roots in the first academy dedicated exclusively to the sciences, which was founded in Rome in 1603 and now has a membership of 80 eminent scientists. Soon after the election of a new Pope named after St Francis of Assisi, Benjamin Ferns relocates the Academy to the City of London, which is synonymous with financial greed. In contrast to the banal, burly modernism of banking, the Academy learns from the Baroque. The densely articulated spatial network and theatrical play of light and shadow set the scene for ideas to form and develop. Learning develops deliberately in public lecture spaces and also by chance as city workers pass over, under and through the building, becoming inadvertent witnesses and collaborators in the new moral debate. The monochrome palette of hatched travertine and articulated basalt focuses attention on perception and learning, accentuating the red and gold papal robes.

Benjamin Ferns, *Pontifical Academy of Sciences,* 2015. Long elevation.

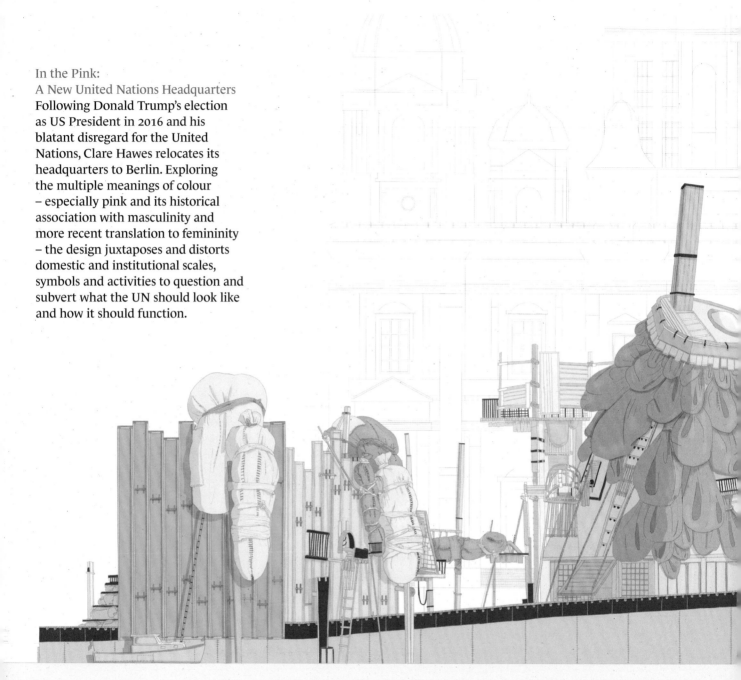

In the Pink:
A New United Nations Headquarters
Following Donald Trump's election as US President in 2016 and his blatant disregard for the United Nations, Clare Hawes relocates its headquarters to Berlin. Exploring the multiple meanings of colour – especially pink and its historical association with masculinity and more recent translation to femininity – the design juxtaposes and distorts domestic and institutional scales, symbols and activities to question and subvert what the UN should look like and how it should function.

Clare Hawes, *In the Pink: A New United Nations Headquarters*, 2017. River elevation.

Left: Boon Yik Chung, *A Portrait of London*, 2018. The Human Menagerie.

Right: Boon Yik Chung, *A Portrait of London*, 2018. The Modern Day Ophelia.

A Portrait of London

Learning from the intersection of architecture and painting – a history that is largely ignored by contemporary architects – Boon Yik Chung reactivates paint as a design medium and building material. A tragicomedy, *A Portrait of London* conceives architecture as a commentary on the human condition, exposing social tension and existential angst. Complex spatial and temporal illusions blur the line between what is solid, reflected or painted, real or semi-real. All the architectural elements – whether chairs, windows or people – are understood figuratively as characters illustrating personal stories. Immersed and absorbed in each interior scene, we observe the figures voyeuristically, and they look back at us.

London Physic Gardens: A New Necropolis

Offering the end-of-life meaningful expression and regenerative potential, nutrients derived from resomation – water cremation – feed a botanical garden and verdant necropolis. Addressing multiple scales – from a plant to a city – and their seasonal interactions, Sam Coulton acknowledges linear and cyclical conceptions of time. Discarding morbid black, the project is indebted to the ruminations on life, death and the immaterial in *International Klein Blue* and Derek Jarman's subsequent film *Blue*, 1993.[5] The colour is imprinted in built fabric and shrouds of the deceased, and profuse in flowers. Blue effluent seeps into the river and groundwater, leaving stains that ebb and flow as an expression of personal and public mourning. Condensation and mist enliven the stark pallor of a Portland stone facade and the white chest fur of a feral fox also adopts a blue tinge.

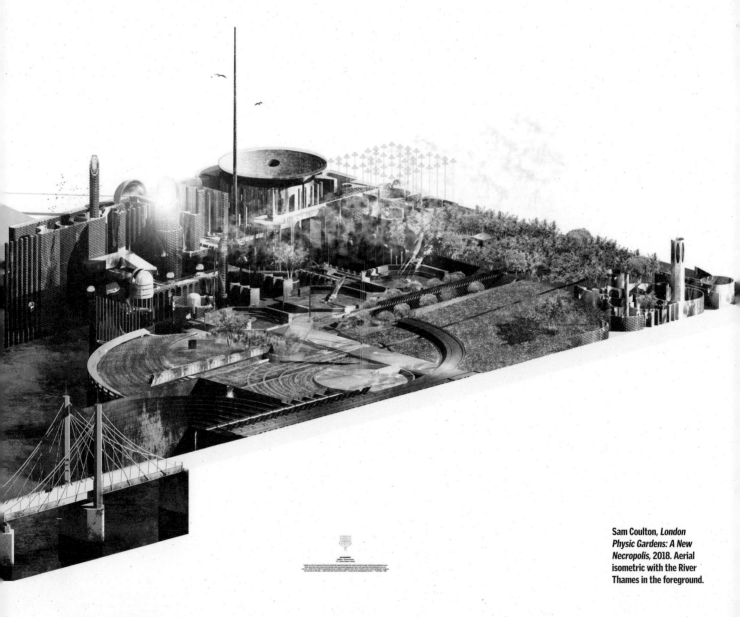

Sam Coulton, *London Physic Gardens: A New Necropolis,* **2018. Aerial isometric with the River Thames in the foreground.**

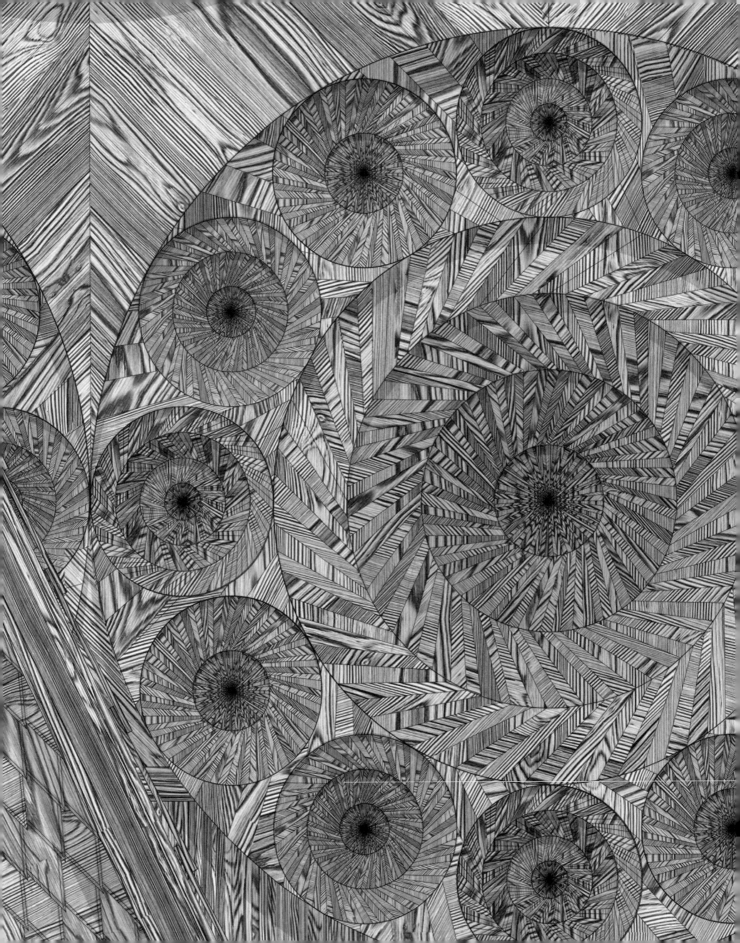

The Woodland Parliament

Sweden is rooted in the forest – physically and emotionally. In response to the renovation of the national parliament building, Elin Söderberg relocates the Riksdagshus from central Stockholm to a dense forest at the urban periphery, accessible only by foot or boat. Drawing on primitive memories of the forest in the Swedish psyche and imagination, traditional timber architecture and modern construction methods combine to herald a sustainable building future and a new approach to government. Op Art timber motifs are set against the potentially more sinister agendas that play out within the forest, amongst fairy tales and politics.

Elin Söderberg, *The Woodland Parliament*, 2018. Entrance elevation.

The Origins of Architecture and the 2050 UN Climate Summit

Conceiving the origins of architecture as one of the most stimulating, recurring design questions led Dominic Walker to appreciate Neolithic Orkney and the continuing relevance of an ancient architecture in which ways of making and being were interdependent. Reforestation returns Orkney to its early human condition. An island site at the edge of the archipelago utilises the rising sea levels and fragile causeway to invoke urgency, isolation and peril, housing a research institute to host the 2050 UN Climate Summit. Carving into the island and building within and above the quarries, the construction techniques and materials – sandstone, concrete and timber – suggest differing degrees of enclosure and permanence. Continually under construction, the project implies a new beginning as well a future ruin – a tomb to the end of architecture – emphasising that human history is minuscule in comparison to that of the Earth.

Dominic Walker, *The Origins of Architecture and the 2050 UN Climate Summit*, 2019. Aerial view.

Laura Keay, *The New English Rural*, 2020. The seasonal clock.

The New English Rural

In response to anthropogenic climate change and post-Brexit agricultural policy, Laura Keay reassesses ruralism as a means to value local resources, develop seasonal appreciation, minimise waste, reduce travel and critique neoliberal capitalism, thus gaining economic, environmental, social and architectural benefits. A prototype for site-specific rural communities in other English regions, the testbed is a deprived brownfield site adjacent to the River Medway. Laura concludes that old rather than new technologies are the most appropriate and innovative tools for a new rural architecture.[6] Nothing goes to waste, and every building component has a history of repair and reuse. Developed during the first Covid-19 lockdown, the project's make-do-and-mend ethos is notably expressed in the 'Bic Biro', singularly employing a humble, everyday tool to create detailed, evocative drawings.

Above: Isaac Nanabeyin Simpson,
*An Architecture Between Culture,
The Highland Council*, 2020.
Constructing the vessel.

Below: Isaac Nanabeyin Simpson,
*An Architecture Between Culture,
The Highland Council*, 2020. The
roaming vessel.

An Architecture Between Culture, The Highland Council

Inverting dominant history, Isaac Nanabeyin Simpson maps the African gaze onto the British landscape to generate a hybrid space between them, avoiding cultural binaries to facilitate conversation rather than difference. Challenging the most unequal landownership in the Western world, the project gradually transforms the Scottish Highlands according to a collective farming model redolent of West Africa. Each year, in the season of rebirth – Spring – the four commissions of the Highland Council meet at their Fort William base to devise annual synergies between the deer, sheep, land and forests. Exploiting the Scottish 'right to roam', a migratory vessel with sacrificial and reusable elements slowly traverses the Highlands, applying the annual farming policy and adopting the social purpose of collective labour observed in traditional West African mud architecture. Allegorical as well as literal, the vessel represents the nomadic movement of culture itself, hauled across borders, reconstructing the Highlands according to the conversations of commissions and communities.

Histories of the future

A design Unit depends to a considerable degree on the challenging and inventive work of its students, but its purpose is also to imagine, nourish and sustain the creative life and exciting projects that follows graduation. One notable consequence is an international community of friends and colleagues in academia and practice. Celebrating the continuing relevance of historical understanding to design and telling compelling stories through the medium of architecture, Unit 12 is an ever-evolving collective history, critically and creatively reinterpreting the past – including its own – in order to reimagine the future.

Until 2017, Unit 12 was tutored by Matthew Butcher, Elizabeth Dow and Jonathan Hill.
Since 2018, the tutors are Elizabeth Dow and Jonathan Hill.

1   Denys Lasdun, 'The Architecture of Urban Landscape' in *Architecture in an Age of Scepticism: A Practitioner's Anthology Compiled by Denys Lasdun*, ed. D. Lasdun, London, Heinemann, 1984, p 137.
2   Lennard J. Davis, *Factual Fictions: The Origins of the English Novel*, Philadelphia, University of Pennsylvania Press, 1996, first published in 1983.
3   Fiona Harvey, 'Global Heating: London to Have Climate Similar to Barcelona by 2050', *The Guardian*, https://www.theguardian.com/environment/2019/jul/10/global-heating-london-similar-climate-barcelona-2050, 10 July 2019, (accessed 30 July 2020); The Crowther Lab ETH Zürich, 'Cities of the Future: Visualizing Climate Change to Inspire Action', https://crowtherlab.pageflow.io/cities-of-the-future-visualizing-climate-change-to-inspire-action? (accessed 30 July 2020).
4   John Evelyn, *Fumifugium: Or, The Inconveniencie of the Aer, and Smoake of London Dissipated*, London, B. White, 1772, pp 3, 28, 34–37, 47–49, first published in 1661 with a slightly different title; John Evelyn, *Sylva, or A Discourse of Forest-Trees, and the Propagation of Timber in His Majesties Dominions*, London, Royal Society, 1664, pp 112–120.
5   Yves Klein identified *International Klein Blue* in the late 1950s.
6   David Edgerton, *The Shock of the Old: Technology and Global History Since 1900*, London, Profile, 2008, p 212.

The Architectural History of Civilisation and My Design

Terunobu Fujimori

Translation by Rei Sawaki

In order to widely and deeply research the course of modern Japanese architecture that started with the Meiji Restoration in 1868, I have been 'walking', 'seeing', 'thinking' and 'writing' about architectures around the world, starting from the Stone Age, via the Bronze Age, to the twentieth century CE, for 50 years. Besides that pursuit of architectural history, I began architectural design 28 years ago, which leads me here today. In this endeavour, I have reached the following understandings of the architectural history of civilisation:

1. The interior space of architecture started with the cave wall paintings for worshipping Mother Earth in the Paleolithic period. The facade of architecture derives from the pillars for worshipping the sun in the Neolithic period.
2. The caves as Mother Earth and the pillars as Father Sky began in Europe and reached America through Asia. We can barely see any different characteristics for each region, so we can conclude that they were universal.
3. The interior space and facade began to integrate at the end of the Neolithic period, and here we can see the beginning of architecture. However, few examples exist, and only the Megalithic Temples of Malta give a glimpse of the original state.
4. Different religions, philosophies, characters and arts began to emerge in different areas, such as Egypt, the Middle East, India and China, in the Bronze Age. This is the start of architectural history for each region.

Therefore, the appropriate narrative of architectural history is not to start from the pyramids but the holy caves of the Paleolithic period and distinguish that from the Bronze Age. The world before the Paleolithic period was universal, and it became individualistic with the Bronze Age. Each region around the world developed separately, and this is why architectural history is rich and diverse. However, this individualism ended in the nineteenth century. The last period of this long, long architectural journey is called 'Historicist Architecture'. Initiating the next era, Art Nouveau, including the Arts and Crafts movement, is the beginning of Modernism, which was properly established with the Bauhaus building in 1926. My understanding of Modernism is explained here:

1. The Reason for the Formation of Modernism

I believe that the new age of Modernism, which continues today, started with the two modern principles of 'Science and Technology' born from the Industrial Revolution and 'Civic Society' initiated by the French Revolution. When you think about the reason why Modernism was born a century after the Industrial Revolution and French Revolution, I cannot help but sense deep-rooted resistance in the conscious and unconscious minds of architects that prohibited them from following Modernist principles. From the Paleolithic period, religion was always the driving force for creating a new architectural expression. Although in Europe, the Renaissance relativised the absolute authority of religion and the number of secular building types increased, religion as a motive never went away; it changed its appearance and remained in the depths of the architect's mind. What finished off this ethos of architects that remained like a tailbone? Friedrich Nietzsche's 1883 statement: 'God is Dead.'[1] Architectural history does not usually connect Nietzsche's proclamation with the birth of Modernism, but it makes sense as a zeitgeist if God died in 1883 and Art Nouveau emerged immediately after. Leaving the debate of whether God actually died or not to one side, I cannot believe that architects, who seek to become the advocates for their period, stopped pursuing a principle that gives birth to, supports and yet transcends our world. If so, what was the principle that allowed architects to not fall into Nihilism and became the catalyst for creating architecture? Technology replaced God.

2. The Formation of Modernism

It is a little over 30 years from the emergence of Art Nouveau to the completion of the Bauhaus building. Although it is a short period, you realise that various things occurred in sequence: structure, plan and design progressed independently. Let's start with structure. Between steel and reinforced concrete, I will focus on reinforced concrete, which is unique to the modern era. It derived from the patent invented by the French gardener Joseph Monier in 1867, which was acquired by the German company Wayss & Freytag in 1887. It is a structural technology in which steel deals with tension, whereas concrete copes with compression. However, as we see in Theodor Fischer's Pauluskirche in Ulm, 1911, reinforced concrete then just meant bricks stacked between reinforced concrete frames and the concrete surface shaved off with a chisel. The breakthrough was the Église Notre-Dame du Raincy, 1923, the world's first fully exposed concrete structure, designed by the French architect Auguste Perret. This influenced the Reinanzaka House, 1926, by Antonin Raymond in Japan and perhaps led to the Pavillon Suisse, 1930, by Le Corbusier in France. Thereafter, the exposed reinforced concrete structure was firmly established as Modernism's typical construction. So what about plans? One of Modernism's main aims was to transform cellular rooms into fluid space. The first to tackle this theme was the American architect Frank Lloyd Wright, who was strongly influenced by the Japanese traditional open-plan space of the Phoenix Palace *(Hooden)* at the 1893 World's Columbian Exposition in Chicago. Wright encapsulated the continuity and integration of space in the *Wasmuth Portfolio*, 1910, published in Germany. Walter Gropius and Ludwig Mies van der Rohe became aware of the directivity of plans and elevations through this book, as seen in Gropius' Fagus Factory, 1911. This development influenced De Stijl and led to Gerrit Rietveld's Schröder House, Utrecht, 1924, which is a three-dimensional composition of white walls, and later Gropius' Bauhaus building.

3. The Extinction of Historicism

When a new architecture emerges, there is always the extinction of an old architecture. The Historicist themes of 'style', 'decoration' and 'texture' became the opponent for Modernism to defeat. The young architects who distanced themselves from Historicism first broke away from the Gothic Revival and Neoclassicism. Although the specific styles disappeared, unfettered decoration remained in the total system of style, and the architecture that highlighted this the most was Art Nouveau. When you look at Otto Wagner's Majolica House, Vienna, 1890, you realise that the floral decoration spreads throughout the facade, ignoring the distinctive elements of window, column and wall. Decoration existed in Historicism, but it never deviated in this way. What comes to the surface when the decoration of Art Nouveau disappears? Texture, as you can see in the brick walls of the Technical Administration

Building of Hoechst AG, 1924, by Peter Behrens. The architecture that scraped off the last remaining texture was the white wall of De Stijl and the Bauhaus. Historicism disappeared, and each style, decoration and texture ended in sequence. The independently born aspects of Modernism, such as reinforced concrete, continuous plan, free-flowing elevation, white wall and geometrical composition all came together in the Bauhaus, creating the 'white box with large glass'.

4. After the Bauhaus

Let's trace the movement around the world after 1926. It spreads from Germany to Europe, then to the United States and Japan, but immediately a different group of architects emerges. They agree with the basic principles of Modernism, but their passions cannot be contained within the 'white box with large glass'. The first of these architects is Le Corbusier, who identified with the Bauhaus at first, but after the Pavillon Suisse transitioned to an architecture of free form, exposed concrete and stone finishes. The first to notice Le Corbusier's transition was the young Kenzō Tange. His graduation project CHATEAU D'ART, 1938, references the curved surfaces and stone finishes of the Pavillon Suisse, His thesis, 'Ode to Michelangelo: As an Introduction to the Study of Le Corbusier', 1939, justly distinguishes Gropius from Le Corbusier after the Pavillon Suisse, using the Japanese translation of Martin Heidegger's 'Hölderlin and the Essence of Poetry', 1938.[2] Tange condemns Gropius' forms as under the control of the 'geometry of death',[3] and criticises white box architecture as 'sanitary ware (=toilet)',[4] specifically criticising the work of Japanese architect Mamoru Yamada, which was included in the 'Modern Architecture: International Exhibition' at the Museum of Modern Art, New York, 1932.[5] Le Corbusier deviated from the Bauhaus, whereas Mies accompanied Gropius but did not adopt the white box. Mies' Villa Tugendhat, Brno, 1930, is an architecture with craft quality, with the highest grade marble, and chrome plating covering the steel structure. How should we understand these Modernist masters' departure from the Bauhaus? I believe the key lies in the climate and tradition that influenced them when they were young. For Le Corbusier, it was the Mediterranean scenery of sea, rock and sky that led to the curved free form and stone texture. For Mies, it was the keen sense for texture that

Kenzō Tange. CHATEAU D'ART, 1938. Courtesy, Terunobu Fujimori.

CHATEAU D'ART

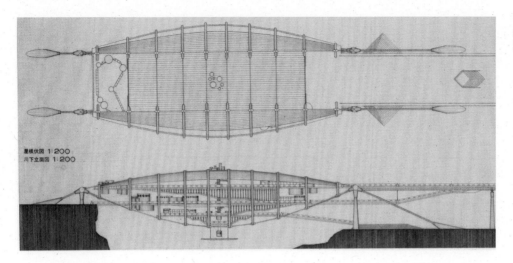

Terunobu Fujimori, 'Bridge: Examining the methods of the visionary architect Ledoux', 1970.

屋根伏図 1:200
川下立面図 1:200

he acquired from his father, who was a stonemason, and the German classicism of Karl Friedrich Schinkel. Tange's asymmetrical building layout derives from the Horyuji Temple, and his structural aesthetic of exposed concrete comes from traditional timber buildings. For Alvar Aalto, the climate of Scandinavia influenced his delicate yet robust style. If you include the period before the Bauhaus, the American prairie and forms of the frontier period influenced Wright, the traditions of Spain influenced Antoni Gaudi, and the Scottish climate influenced Charles Rennie Mackintosh. There can be as many Modernisms as there are climates and cultures in the world.

When you line up the five architectural masters in the order of their contribution to Modernism – Gropius, Mies, Le Corbusier, Wright and Antoni Gaudi – the actual number of people visiting their buildings is completely the opposite. Modernism may be the first expression in architectural history when the evaluation of professionals and people do not match.

In my rough sketch of architectural history, civilisation has twice created from scratch a non-practical architecture with no traditions or precedents. First, in the Stone Age with wood and stone. Second, in the twentieth century with steel, concrete and glass. Both natural and industrial materials have no nationality, which is why each became a global phenomenon. Between the two knots of international architecture in the Stone Age and twentieth century, there were diverse and rich architectures born from the religion, culture, art and tradition of each nation, like a candy wrapped in paper.

Next, I will describe my architectural design work, which is based on the historical understandings summarised above. To be precise, the relations between the 'historical understandings' and the 'designs' are complex, so it is more accurate to say that my design and research mutually influenced each other and led to my perception today. When I was studying architecture at university, I was more interested in design, so I read books and monographs, focusing on Claude Nicolas Ledoux, Le Corbusier, Seiichi Shirai, Arata Isozaki and Archigram. My graduation project was entitled 'Bridge: Examining the methods of the visionary architect Ledoux', 1970. It was a project in which the greenery of the riverbank takes revenge on the city, and I placed a spaceship-like bridge over the river that had recovered clean water and lush vegetation. However, for my Master's degree, I stopped designing and wrote a history. I travelled around Japan and the West and obtained some of the historical understandings I have already touched on. The two-volume *Modern Architecture of Japan* was published in 1993. Before this, my first project Jinchōkan Moriya Historical Museum was completed in 1991, and ever since I have continued both historical research and design. There was a family called Moriya in the small mountain village where I was born and brought up. The Moriya family worshipped the Moriya-mountain as a god, a tradition that can be traced back to before the beginning of farming. Associated with the hunting era, religious rituals include dedicating to God two bloody frogs stabbed with an arrow, staying inside a pit dwelling during winter and coming out in spring to eat 'deer meat with brains' and 'grilled boar skin' with local people. The village decided to create a historical museum for the Moriya family to preserve the customs of the Jomon Neolithic period, and they consulted me on its architecture. I had close relationships with my contemporary architects, such as Toyo Ito, Tadao Ando and Osamu Ishiyama, but their philosophy and design

Right: Stone House,
Portugal. Photograph,
Terunobu Fujimori.

did not match the traditions of the Jomon period, so I decided to design it myself, establishing two conditions:

1. To make the design different from any country or style. If someone views it as a design by a historian, they will stop thinking about the architecture itself.
2. To make it different to Modernism. Modernism does not match the Jomon period, and would destroy the natural environment and scenery. If I designed a Modernist building, I knew my contemporaries would stop treating my work seriously, since I have touched on diverse historical architectures from all over the world in my writings.

However, I immediately reached a dead end when I started designing with these two conditions. When I sketched something, the images of Modernism, the traditional forms of Japanese architecture and the masterpieces I visited in Europe and the United States came out. The experience of visiting architectures of all times and places as a historian got in my way as a designer. I could not go back in time or look at my contemporaries, nor look at the architectures of the West or the East. Since I decided to not follow any style of any culture, I could not figure out how to create a shape anymore. My breakthrough was the text of Takamasa Yoshizaka, who studied under Le Corbusier immediately after the war, in which he writes about the 'House of Mud' that he saw in north-east China when he was a Master's student: 'It is a primitive house standing alone in the dry grassland, with no windows or roofs. You can only notice it is a dwelling from its entrance.'[6] With this short sentence, I was able to escape architectural history from the Bronze Age to Modernism. I realise now that the 'House of Mud' took me to the Paleolithic and Neolithic period, which was the first international

architectural era built with soil, wood, grass and stone. I believe any expressive act of humanity is fundamentally international. Only the Paleolithic and Neolithic period and Modernism have this international expression. That is why I aim to design things that do not belong to any country or style. I have encountered three buildings that share the quality of the 'House of Mud' that Yoshizaka captured with his sentence. The region, era and scale are all different. They are the Stone House in Portugal, Seaweed Roof House in Denmark and Tsubokawa-ke House in Japan, which respectively date from around the 1970s, eighteenth century and seventh century.

When, led by the 'House of Mud', I decided to adopt the first international style for the shape of the Moriya Museum, a new problem emerged: structure. Only earthquake and fire resistant architecture built with reinforced concrete or steel is allowed for buildings that house cultural assets. A timber structure was impossible. One of the principles of Modernism is the 'unity of structure, material and expression'. If I followed this rule, I would foolishly exhibit the Jomon period in an exposed concrete or steel space. For an architectural historian, brought up in the nature-worshipping environment protected by the Moriya family, it feels almost like a mental sin to do that. Subverting the words of Adolf Loos, 'Modernism is a crime.'[7] Through these dilemmas, the desperate solution of installing soil, grass, wood and stone on the surface of the reinforced concrete structure was invented. The strong, homogeneous, industrial material was hidden in the back, whereas the weak, diverse, natural material was in the front for people to see. Carefully selecting materials that enhanced my concept, I highlighted the natural diversity of the soil, grass, wood and stone. For soil, I added grass to make it rougher. For

Above: Seaweed Roof House,
Denmark. Photograph,
Terunobu Fujimori

Designs on History: The Architect as Physical Historian

wood, I chose pieces that had more knots, cracks and uneven grain. For stone, I used the most natural. With the ideas and methods described above, the Moriya Museum was born. The whole image of the architecture is inspired by Yoshizaka's 'House of Mud'. The texture of the soil wall comes from the neighbouring henhouse that has an old-style soil wall mixed with sand, the roof finish is a stone commonly used for the farmhouses of the area, and the wooden boards on the wall imitate the traditional 'rain protection' of the house next door. The interior floor, wall and ceiling are painted like a cave. The openings look like holes in a cave. Looking at the facade when most of the building was completed, I realised that the mono-pitched roof resembled a Hokora, a small shrine, and tried to deviate from that image. Considering different options, my pencil accidentally slipped. I thought 'this is it!'. The timber column going through the stone roof is a yew tree cut down in the village. For the people of the area to accept this unusual design, I referred to the Onbashira pillar festival celebrated by the Moriya family, but actually it does not follow that. The wooden board covering the soil wall was the part I struggled with the most. Through my knowledge of architectural history, I knew that boards were not cut with a saw, but were split with a stone or metal tool found everywhere around the world before

Medieval times. So I wanted to use a split board. Looking everywhere and trying it myself, I came across an old craftsman who had done this before the war, and asked him to split the long wooden boards. I observed these building techniques in the neighbourhood of the site, but you can see similar ones all around the world. After completion, I was most worried that 'wrapping nature around technology' would look fake. Luckily, it looked like proper architecture in my eyes, and no one said that the natural materials seemed light or cheap. Osamu Ishiyama and Kengo Kuma quickly responded:

It is clear that this architecture is envisioned in a situation with abundant nature … This small architecture is filled with sharp criticism of the situation of today's architecture … It is an architecture that should last long in people's memory.[8] Osamu Ishiyama

Fujimori created an extremely anachronist object that is difficult to describe or compare, that does not belong to any kind of 'past' nor 'countryside'. The vast 'anti-modernistic knowledge' of an architectural historian, on the contrary, led him to reject a simple anti-modern attitude. Therefore that whole idea is represented in nature as a criticism of contemporary architecture.[9] Kengo Kuma

Left: Tsubokawa-ke House, Japan. Photograph, Terunobu Fujimori.

My architectural design work started in this way, but its philosophy and methods have not changed. Later, I added the theme of 'architectural greening' and the tearoom building type. I formed Rojo Kansatsu Gakkai (Society for Observing the Streets) with Gempei Akasegawa and Shinbo Minami in 1986, before my first project. One of the unique buildings we collected while walking around the city was the 'Street Botanical Garden', and I came up with an idea of 'finishing the surface of a skyscraper with dandelions' while we talked about the relations between the city and plants. Here, my interest in architectural greening was born. Since then I have researched the history and current situation of architectural greening in Japan and around the world and tested the idea in my second project, my own home, Dandelion House, 1995, and my third project, Leek House, 1997, for Akasegawa, continuing with the idea without being discouraged by failures. The long history of architectural greening began with the legendary Hanging Gardens of Babylon. Among the buildings I have visited, notable examples are the seventeenth-century Guinigi Tower in Lucca, Italy, Akita Shoukai, 1915, in Japan, Lucio Costa and Oscar Niemeyer's Ministry of Education and Health Building, 1943, in Rio de Janeiro, Brazil, which follows the idea

Above: Terunobu Fujimori,
Dandelion House, Japan, 1995.

Below: Terunobu Fujimori,
The Grass Roof, Japan, 2015.

of Le Corbusier's roof garden, and the traditional turf roofs of France and Japan. However, typical contemporary examples are disappointing because the greening and the architecture are not aesthetically integrated. For me, architectural greening started as a joke or dream of 'finishing the surface of a skyscraper with dandelions', but it was an idea that came from my interest in the cracks between nature and architecture that developed with the Industrial Revolution. So, in my graduation project the river strikes back at the city and in my first project I attempted to 'wrap nature around technology'. Ever since, I have tested numerous methods of greening, but most of the time the result is troubling for the client.

In describing the use of natural materials and architectural greening in my designs, I note the success of the former and the continuing failure of the latter. However, I luckily succeeded in stopping my failures in two recent projects: The Grass Roof, 2015, and Mosaic Tile Museum, 2017. I wrapped the buildings with natural materials, and the architectural greening also was a success. The greenery was separated from the ground and covered all of the roof, in which windows were placed. With these three methods, I succeeded in integrating architecture and greenery.

1 Friedrich Nietzsche, *The Gay Science*, trans. W. Kaufmann, New York, Vintage Books, 1974, p 181; first published as *Die Fröhliche Wissenschaft* in 1882. Refer to Friedrich Nietzsche, *Thus Spake Zarathustra*, trans T. Common, Edinburgh, Foulis, 1909; first published between 1883–85.
2 When Tange was studying at Tokyo University, he distanced himself from Marxism due to the oppression of Marxist scholars and tried to deeply rethink Modernist architecture. He became fascinated not by the Bauhaus or Gropius but by Le Corbusier's work after the Pavillon Suisse and began to consider the difference between the Bauhaus and Le Corbusier. Kenzō Tange and Terunobu Fujimori, *Kenzō Tange*, Tokyo, Shinkenchiku, 2002.
3 Kenzō Tange, 'Ode to Michelangelo: As an Introduction to the Study of Le Corbusier', *Gendai Kenchiku*, December 1939, p 40.
4 It is widely known that Tange used to talk in this way about Gropius back then. When I asked Tange about it he answered: 'The praise for Gropius was so high in Japan that it was impossible for me to write about him in an ill manner. Gropius looked after me in America after the war, so I could not talk ill about such a thoughtful person.'
5 Curated by Henry-Russell Hitchcock and Philip Johnson.
6 For the 'House of Mud' text, refer to Takamasa Yoshizaka, *Yoshizaka Takamasa shu*, vol 4, Tokyo, Keiso shobo, 1986, p 6.
7 Loos' essay 'Ornament and Crime' was first published in 1908. Adolf Loos, *Ornament and Crime: Selected Essays*, trans. M. Mitchell, Riverside CA, Ariadne Press, 1997.
8 Osamu Ishiyama, 'Abundant Nature in Harmony', *Shinkenchiku*, June 1991, p 127.
9 Kengo Kuma, 'Something Never Seen Before But Feels Nostalgic', *Kenchiku Broucher 001 Jinchōkan Moriya Historical Museum*, 1992, p 31

Terunobu Fujimori, Mosaic Tile Museum, Japan, 2017.

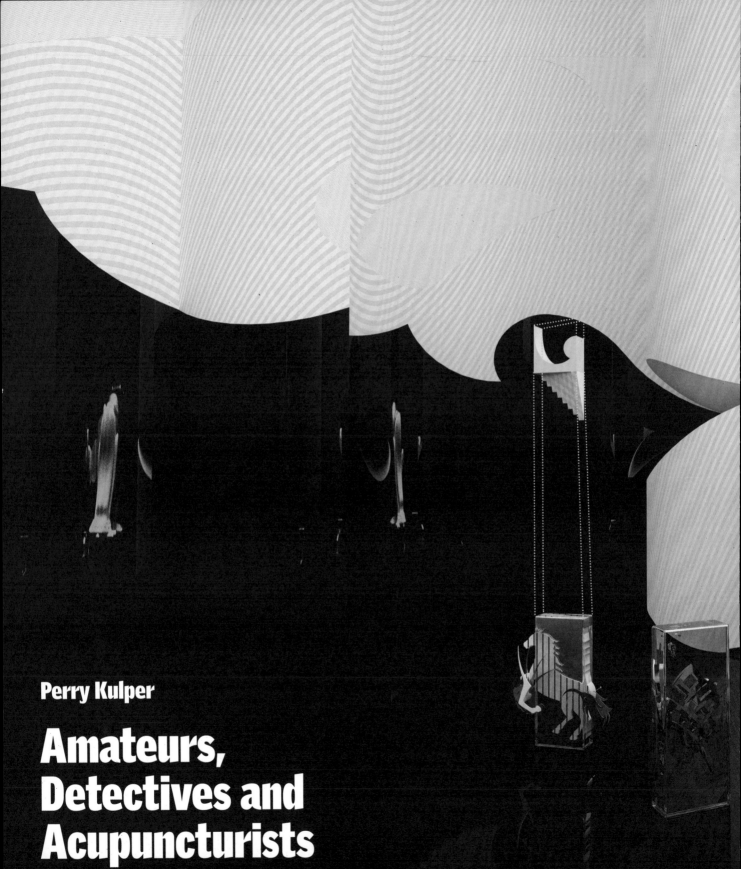

Perry Kulper

Amateurs,
Detectives and
Acupuncturists

Yiran Zhao, *Canary'ed Yellow: Spontaneous Forms*, 2020.

Daunting, pithy and exhilarating; history is a moving target. Tantalisingly complex, its roles, capacities and translations pulse, and at times convulse, reflexively. As emphatically underscored by recent global protests against structural racism, histories as cultural barometers are explicit, implicit, hidden, manufactured and misrepresented – many in urgent need of rewriting, or flat-out abandonment. And while architecture inevitably participates in the history of ideas – knowingly, or not, these historical constructions are proffered from value-laden perspectives that are often indefinite, incomplete and inaccurate in their range, inclusion and depiction. Histories are vagabonds, attempting to outrun the voracious appetite for certainty, quantification and all-knowing empowerment. And, consequently, disempowerment.

These thoughts are penned by an amateur, etymologically rooted in Greek philosophy, and in cultural values that enabled athletes to compete in the Olympic Games – the amateur is at times a productive design ally, striking a balance between intent and open-minded passion. Pointing to relations of history and design, these thoughts tickle: the history of ideas and representation; two pivotal books; the roles that history might play; tactics and strategies frequently leveraged; and historically grounded authoring positions.

University of Michigan student work, and an in-progress project of mine, are both curated à la Argentinian short-story writer, poet and translator Jorge Luis Borges' 'Celestial Emporium of Benevolent Knowledge', 1942, which plays the role of a metaphorical field guide, lightly framing history and design as related to teaching and creative practice.[1]

Five 'other' points

The discipline of architecture is inextricably stitched to a richly embroidered history of ideas – structured through myriad disciplines, forms of cultural reflection and production. In design, historical affiliations tickle developments in optics, geometry, mathematics, religion and philosophy, to name a few. These deep trajectories frame cultural, spatial and practised continuities. Speculatively, the construction of ideas might be unhinged from known epistemological models, altering historical accounts, instead becoming temporally promiscuous – rebooting and transforming its DNA. And arguably, acupuncture-like awareness about relations to the history of ideas offers the possibility that design can be enriched by, and co-constructed by and with those histories, participatorily – prompting a generative cultural play between deep continuities and explosive change.

Implicitly, representation is a navigational prop for designers. Developments of linear perspective, accelerated and decelerated perspective, anamorphic and parallel projections, photography, film, and now virtual reality and artificial intelligence, animate, arguably dictate, what is possible, philosophically, conceptually, spatially and representationally. The power of representation is undeniable, epitomised in the mathematisation of linear perspective where the authorial supremacy of the self – the 'I', 'station point eye', 'point of view' and 'world view' – implicitly takes on god-like ownership of a constructed world articulated on a picture plane, relinquishing the virtues, and even necessity, of living in the world. In parallel, the architectural drawing is motivated by ideas, on one hand, and by material make up, or construction, on another, implicitly tangoing with assumptions about negotiations between drawn surfaces, or pixels of speculation, and construction, or building. But what those rapidly changing relations are, and what they mean, must not be taken for granted. As the roles and definitions of the architect transform, exponentially, so too may the loaded roles and consequential histories of spatial representation.

Written and illustrated works – whether manifestos, treatises, fact or fiction, remain critical to design. Swiss-French architect Le Corbusier's *Vers une architecture*, 1923, advocated learning from the past, while advancing a kind of noble purism – acknowledging the influence of white Greek temples on his work.[2] Earlier, his proposal for the Maison Domino, 1914, established tabula rasa values, effectively erasing the grounds of history, by raising the diagrammatic house above a newly constructed ground like a Phoenix. American architect Robert Venturi's *Complexity and Contradiction in Architecture*, 1966, his 'gentle manifesto', also promoted lessons from the past.[3] Some 350 images of architectural examples from across millennia frame varied relations to history, while foregrounding his interest in Mannerism, 'both/and', and the difficult whole. Read in graduate school, subsequent to Le Corbusier's writing and framing of architecture and new culture, this work tickled my appetite for design opportunities, when relevant, to historical references. The values positioned in both books opened the conceptual floodgates – animating varied ways to refer to 'a past', challenging default tabula rasa assumptions. These books foreground design strategies and history, effectively increasing the conceptual and communicative scope of architecture – perhaps participatorily, through time.

Equally, history can play roles in design, including the rhetorical, discursive, associative and analogical, to name a few – relations to history can critically reframe values embedded in spatial realms, rerouting default assumptions. Akin to the roles of sites, and programmes, relations to history can be advantageous in acts of design, enriching the pool from which relations are structured, and meaningful experiences had. Similarly, the design strategies and tactics deployed, with respect to history, are multiple, including fakes and copies, staunch historic preservation, adaptive reuse, planned obsolescence and tabula rasa approaches. Alternatively, a generative use of history can enable spatial and representational relations, constructing new knowledge, rather than simply adhering to what is known.

In design terms, leveraging historically grounded forms of authorship enables a broadened range of subject positions and audience constructions. The authoring promise of the amateur, alongside that of the detective – sniffing out the territory, the acupuncturist – on the hunt for hidden but effective relations, and even the innocent bystander – keeping things honest through indifference,

are useful protagonists in my practice. Authoring positions can radically alter conceptual, structural and implementational approaches, hinged to choreograph the variables in the practice of designing. First or third person positions, collective and multiple authoring positions, open the creative channels, analogously. Roland Barthes' 'The Death of the Author', 1967, Michel Foucault's 'What Is an Author?', 1969, and Marcel Duchamp's 'The Creative Act', 1957, are useful co-pilots.[4]

On the ground
In addition to the myriad relations to history sketched out above, Borges' 'Celestial Emporium of Benevolent Knowledge', an important historical reference and frequent teaching and practice accomplice, advocates for difference, for heterogeneity – in stark contrast to the streamlined homogeneity of modernity. It is useful, analogously, to frame the student work included here, all taking on the potential uses of history in design. The student accomplishments are coupled with a recent project of mine that frames the historical potential of Netherlandish triptychs, Baroque churches and still life painting, from a design perspective – enabling design research to reframe important cultural references, histories as it were, generatively.

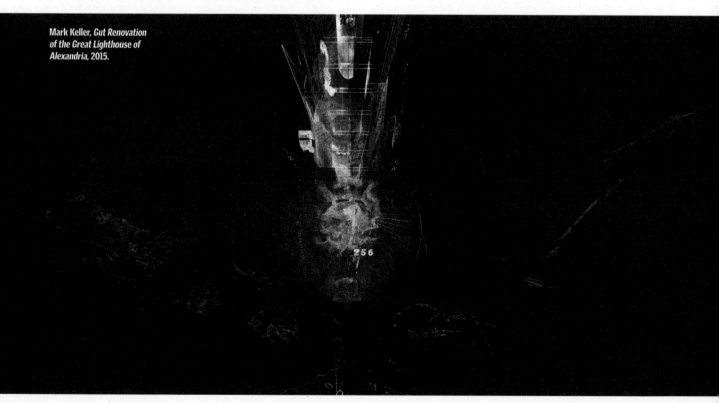

Mark Keller, *Gut Renovation of the Great Lighthouse of Alexandria*, 2015.

Hang-Hyun Cho,
Rogue Ornament, 2017.

Designs on History: The Architect as Physical Historian

Luna Wei, *Beijing Bunny Pagoda*, 2019.

Mark Keller's *Gut Renovation of the Great Lighthouse of Alexandria*, 2015, utilises a historical document, an image of a drawing of the Great Lighthouse of Alexandria, as a rhetorical and representational site. It wonders about the undiscerning night, in search of a more tolerant architecture, one that tickles a tensional play between fact and fiction, in his words, unreconcilably so. The proposition is articulated through a series of spaces intended to activate a narrative response to architectural transparency, a poster child for total control, championed by the likes of René Descartes, Jeremy Bentham and Le Corbusier.

In *Rogue Ornament*, 2017, Hang-Hyun Cho reroutes the historical consequences of ornamentation. Situated in a speculative site – comprised of Adolf Loos' Villa Müller, Prague, 1930, and a subterranean section of St Peter's, Rome – this work ruminates on the loss of the historically important communicative roles of ornamentation. It argues for celebration of ornament production as contemporary performance, grounded ritualistically. Analogically linked to Le Corbusier's 'Five

Points Towards a New Architecture', 1926, the work forms five contemporary 'orders' of ornament production: abstract, connotative, tailored, trompe l'oeil and materiality.[5] These revive the communicative potential of ornament production through a surreal world configured by fabrication methods, historical figures, fantasy, symbolism, framed views, analogical and metaphorical thinking and fragmented clues.

Utilising an analogical design strategy, Luna Wei's *Beijing Bunny Pagoda*, 2019, structures a representational urbanism that remembers losses incurred through the removal of human practices and material spaces – a mimetic urban proposition. Metaphorical bunnies generate machinic pagodas, capable of storing memories, histories, of now non-existent architectures and spatial practices. Analogic reconstructions tickle atmospheres produced by the making of hot dumplings on winter nights, ringing bicycle bells in a narrow hutong and sweet air as related to a frozen winter lake. The rabbits, symbols of fertility, animate their version of a bygone world, populating a pagoda by constructing

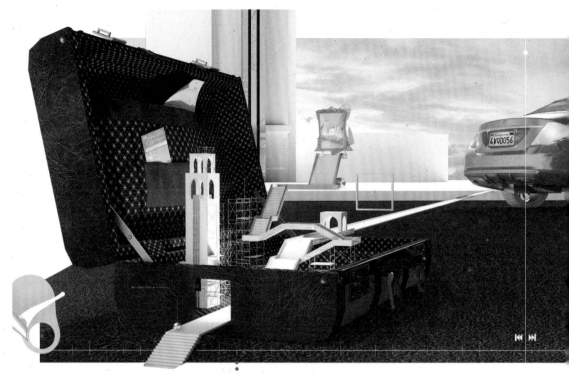

Emily Richards, *(No Vacancy/ Nine Lives of the) Land's End Hotel*, 2019.

Kallie Sternburgh, *Twenty-Five Karats: Authentic Fictions*, 2016.

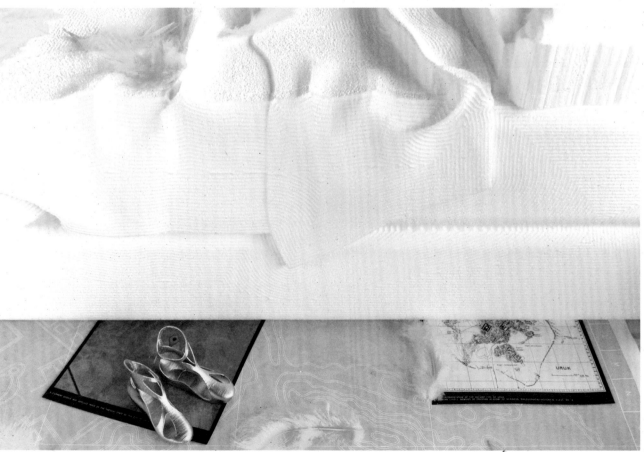

a labyrinthine archive to reconstruct a disappearing Beijing. The proposal leverages an absurd world, in memory of lost practices, architecture and histories, abandoned in the processes of rapid urbanisation.

When construction began for Emily Richards' new (*No Vacancy/ Nine Lives of the*) *Land's End Hotel*, 2019, on the site of old Sutro bathhouse ruins, mysterious hydraulic tunnels, never seen on the civil survey, suddenly appeared. Evidence of rooms that reconstruct themselves, nocturnally, fossils of previous architectures and a phantom bell chiming ritualistically, appeared. Uncanny incidents, choreographed by haunted spatial ghosts, result in a hotel comprised of spatial fragments, and kinds of evidence, architectural, archaeological and mythical. These act as poltergeists, ventriloquists and doppelgangers, critically reframing tabula rasa approaches and the oft-sought, 'always new'. Revealed through a series of curated perspectives, chance encounters and hotel paraphernalia, the *Land's End Hotel* explores the potential of architecture to reveal explicit histories, shifting temporal frameworks and memories,

augmenting the typical roles of typologies while nourishing a cultural imagination.

Kallie Sternburgh's *Twenty-Five Karats: Authentic Fictions*, 2016, is a collection of artefacts – both natural and artificial, fact and fiction, simultaneously given material and fabricated qualities. Rerouted knowledge construction re-evaluates relations to historical content, outmoded forms of documentation and appropriated forms of representation, emblematising the loss of knowledge. Using fragments of a house – Sears and Roebuck archives are a trope for the work itself – she augments varied forms of authorship and communicative potential, using representation as a rhetorical and discursive tool to hijack multiple narratives.

In *re:Quarry'ed*, 2020, Christopher Humphrey probes the generative uses of history, material extraction and invented spatial devices to reveal and construct site narratives. Material removal leaves areas in economic and geologic ruin – cultural and material wastelands replete with hidden potential. This work acts through a series of choreographed narratives in a derelict stone quarry.

Christopher Humphrey, *re:Quarry'ed*, 2020.

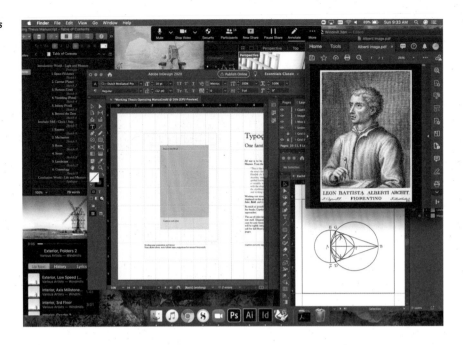

Rangy in scale and task, semi-sentient machinic devices re-quarry, and reconstruct the site, prompting multiple historical, political, cyclical and material complexities. The work is structured through specific devices, characters as it were, that are metaphorically, historically and operationally charged. They co-opt abandoned industrial remnants of the quarry, drawing on mythologies, digital inputs, historic techniques and climatology, to rationalise their respective tasks. The work deploys speciated devices, in a richly embroidered situation, to augment default assumptions about sites, material practices and the deep potential of the roles of making.

Michael Ferguson's *Euclid's Windmill*, 2020, is a reflection on architectural representation, framed through the lenses of art history and literary fiction, laying the foundations for alternative histories and supplemental potential for architectural and spatial vision. It trades on the Italian-led canon of Leon Battista Alberti and his cohort; the Northern Renaissance imagery of Hieronymus Bosch, Pieter Bruegel and Jan van Eyck; pictorial lineages from China, Korea and Japan; and twentieth-century speculative representation techniques. References to windmills play choreographic roles, structuring formal and symbolic resonances, and as a social instrument that gathers disparate farmers. Historically elevated above the landscape, the windmill suggests a shared, social typology, distanced from the history of regal palaces and private residences.

Here, architecture might 'see' otherwise, envisioning alternative political and practised landscapes, acknowledging that a political imaginary is often spatial, and the spatial imaginary is always political.

Burbank, Basilica, Beijing: The Architecture of Metanarrative, 2020, considers mythic (re)constructions by rebooting cultural strongholds of political, spiritual and practiced significance at the Walt Disney Studios in Burbank, California, in 1941. Inspired by the fibreglass fantasies of Disney theme parks, boundaries between the sacred and profane are made ambiguous by scenes choreographed with stage-setting techniques in a big box. The warehouse stage is the site and contains a double of itself – the big box is unfolded and worked on by rogue actors, occupying an analogical drawing table while choreographing distant geographies, utilising Claude Lévi-Strauss' concept of mythological structuralism.[6] Two other locations are implicated in Burbank – St Peter's Basilica and the Terracotta Warriors migrate to a silk painting, a representation of Beijing's Forbidden City, as peony-printed tourists. Deploying filmic and theatrical techniques, disparate mythologies and split-geographies co-exist in a metaphorical wartime operations room, board room, and tabula rasa situation. Sydney Farris' thesis examines the motivations, influences and feedback loops of narrative constructions to affect a reframing of history and cultural legibility, exploiting the deep potential of mythologies.

Sydney Farris, *Burbank,
Basilica, Beijing:
The Architecture of
Metanarrative*, 2020.

Perry Kulper with Kyle Reich,
*Triptychs, Domes + Still
Life(s), Niche*, 2020.

Perry Kulper with Kyle
Reich, Triptychs, *Domes +
Still Life(s), Knolling*, 2020.

Designs on History: The Architect as Physical Historian

Arguably, pervasive and persuasive digital techniques relegate the potential of generating spatial formations to an instrumental, formally constructed, and technologically derived paradigm. Broadening that realm, Yiran Zhao's *Canary'ed Yellow: Spontaneous Forms*, 2020, speculates on a processing system that pixelates and fragments cultural histories, leveraging characteristics of civilisation, spatial realms and lost qualities, translating and hybridising these histories into spliced, but non-collagic, spatial specimens. A three-part system – input scanning, processing-collating and output – genetically, operationally and spatially transform the curated inputs. Hybrid processes fuse the relational structure among the metaphorical parents, reinventing their selected characteristics in search of emergent, and deeply structured, communicative potential. A quasi-real, quasi-invented 'site' – comprised of mimetic heritage ruins and a thirteenth-century Mongolian conquest, all linked to lost civilizations – stages the arrival of newborn species harkening to a reconstruction of temporally 'spent' cultural, spatial and practiced characteristics.

Triptychs, Domes + Still Life(s), a work in progress, 2020, teases 'worlds implicated in other worlds', linked to Netherlandish triptych paintings, Baroque churches and still life painting, leveraging embroidered historical references, to reframe culturally significant forms of production, generatively. Utilising these three parents, metaphorically, analogically and realistically, it probes so-called meaning – how much, and to whom, might significance be communicated, by positioning the same elements in three strategically different situations:

'Still Life: Niche'; 'Knolling' and 'Ryoanji'. The same elements are coupled comparatively, to understand how situational differences afford, reroute and enrich communicative potential. The work asks questions about the 'scope' of work; how much content it can 'hold in play' and augmented uses of historical precedents. The work is linked to broadening the conceptions of architecture and spatial settings, locating meaning at multiple levels in spatial realms, and reflecting, actively, on the consequences of using historical references, spatially and representationally, contemporarily.

Paradoxically, useful and tricky

Architecture, first and foremost, must be generous, activating deep, and often hidden, experiential potential, in human and perhaps non-human species – an active, cultural construction requires this. The traditions, customs, values and embedded potential in history remain critical to the continuities, participation and transformation of architecture. However, history is neither chronological, nor fixed. Sometimes, it's not even known. From this amateur's points of view, we must remain vigilant detectives, cultivating clues about possible negotiations between history and design, to the mutual benefit of both. In equal part, this amateur wouldn't mind being a historical acupuncturist, motivating multiple roles, strategies and tactics or relations to history, in a continual search for a kind of cultural fitness – participating with and constructing, reciprocally, the history of ideas, in their myriad dimensions, towards enriching a cultural imaginary.

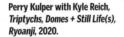

Perry Kulper with Kyle Reich,
Triptychs, Domes + Still Life(s),
Ryoanji, 2020.

1   Jorge Luis Borges, 'El Idioma Analítico de John Wilkins' (The Analytical Language of John Wilkins), https://ccrma.stanford.edu/courses/155/assignment/ex1/Borges.pdf, 1942, (accessed 12 September 2020).
2   Le Corbusier, *Towards a New Architecture*, trans. F. Etchells, London, Architectural Press, 1946, pp 31, 124, 125, 130, 135; first published in English in 1927.
3   Robert Venturi, *Complexity and Contradiction in Architecture*, New York, The Museum of Modern Art, 1966, p 22.
4   Roland Barthes, 'The Death of the Author', in *Image-Music-Text*, trans. S. Heath, London, Flamingo, 1977, pp 142–148; Michel Foucault, 'What is an Author?', trans. J. V. Hariri, in *The Foucault Reader*, ed. P. Rabinow, London, Penguin, 1991. pp 101–120; Marcel Duchamp, 'The Creative Act', http://www.openculture.com/2015/10/hear-marcel-duchamp-read-the-creative-act.html, 1957, (accessed 12 September 2020).
5   Le Corbusier and Pierre Jeanneret, 'Five Points Towards a New Architecture', in *Programs and Manifestoes on 20th Century Architecture*, ed. U. Conrads, trans, M. Bullock, Cambridge MA, MIT Press, 1971, pp 99–101.
6   Claude Lévi-Strauss, *The Way of the Masks*, trans. S. Modelski, Seattle, University of Washington Press, 1982; first published in French in 1975.

Apartheid's Architects

Lesley Lokko

Apartheid-era sign, 'Whites only', c.1979.

Part 1
The Preamble

Email correspondence received 7 July 2020.

Dear Lesley,

Hope you are well.
I was wondering if we could have a conversation
on the use of the word 'apartheid' in the context
of Baltimore's racist urban policies and ensuing
activism. Hope you have time. If not, feel free to
let me know if the word 'apartheid' should/could
be used outside the context of South Africa or not?

Thanks!
Stay well and connected, Samia.[1]

It is not easy to pinpoint the exact date when the word 'apartheid' entered circulation beyond the narrow theological and political debates of South Africa in the 1920s to the 1940s. In 1944, D. F. Malan, speaking as Leader of the Opposition, became the first person to use it in the South African Parliament. 'I do not use the term "segregation"', he stated, 'because it has been interpreted as a fencing off (*afhok*), but rather "apartheid", which will give the various races the opportunity of uplifting themselves on the basis of what is their own.'[2] Four years later, it was sufficiently well-understood by both English- and Afrikaans-speaking South Africans to have been the deciding factor in the outcome of the 1948 election that swept the Nationalist government to power. Although the National Party victory came *after* the end of the Second World War, its potent blend of authoritarian and populist ingredients, together with a fixation on racial purity, has long cemented its association with Nazi ideology and European fascism. But, as the South African scholar Deborah Posel argues, apartheid

cannot be understood as a 'monolithic entity driven by a unitary strategy'.[3] Her assertion, shared by a number of historians, is that there was no single 'grand design', but rather a network of ideologies, events, personalities which contributed towards its blueprint. Hendrik Verwoerd, often referred to as the 'architect of apartheid', formally implemented its policies as Minister of Native Affairs (1950–58), then as Prime Minister (1958–66).

While the origins and etymology of apartheid are key to understanding how this single word has been able to dominate the South African psyche for close to a century, in this article, however, I am more interested in its structural metaphors ('architect', 'grand design', 'blueprint') and in the role of the urban in both constructing and dismantling it. Through the work of three students at the Graduate School of Architecture (GSA), University of Johannesburg, all of whom were born in the early 90s, part of the 'born free' post-apartheid generation, this chapter charts the rise and progress of a new generation of African architects for whom history is neither curse nor covenant.

Part 2

Kgaugelo Lekalakala grew up in her grandmother's house in rural Seabe, Mpumalanga, a three-and-a-half hours' drive from Johannesburg. Her thesis project, supervised by Dr Finzi Saidi, Absalom Makhubu and Dickson Adu-Agyei of Unit 15X at the GSA, entitled *Tales of the Vulnerability of African Women in Transit Spaces*, was published in *City*, in April 2020.[4] In her own words, 'the project uses Surrealist collage-making as a critical architectural tactic to capture and expose the vulnerability of black female bodies in spaces of urban-rural transit'. The project is simultaneously deeply personal and deeply historical, in the way that only a society where history, identity and space have been so tightly intertwined, can produce. To understand the reasons why Lekalakala grew up in her grandmother's house in a rural setting adjacent to, but never part of, the nation's capital, Pretoria, why transit spaces are particularly dangerous for young black women and why traditional architectural methods of enquiry have proved inadequate to the task of exploration requires a different reading and understanding of history. The Group Areas Act (1950, 1957 and 1966) assigned the four different racial groups to separate, strictly enforced areas of both the urban and rural landscape. Along with the Immorality Act (1927, 1957), which prohibited sexual relations between whites and people of 'other' races, apartheid sought to control every possible aspect of a person's life from the macroeconomics of land ownership to the microcosm of intimacy. In South Africa, history cannot be read simply as a narrative of significant events. History is physical, bodily and materially present *in the present*. History is *always* embodied. Twenty-six years after the formal end of apartheid, the vast majority of black South Africans still live in the racially segregated townships (Kasi), usually hours away from their places of employment. In the absence of a formal public transportation network, privately owned taxi-buses (known as 'Combis') are the only means of affordable transport. Unregulated and often desperately overcrowded, they are also unsafe, both on the road and off. As Lekalakala states, 'when women travel back and forth, they are more likely to experience sexual assault. For those of us dependent on such forms of transportation, the entire journey can be daunting. Safety becomes a key consideration, leading to a range of spatial negotiations, compromises and precautionary measures, which greatly limit the experience of mobility as freedom'.[5] In rural settings, where gender roles tend to be more tightly circumscribed, movement in and through space is still highly regulated by notions of behaviour – what constitutes a 'good girl', 'obedient daughters' or 'virtuous apparel'. In the male imaginary, femininity 'is considered static, located firmly within the domestic sphere, while masculinity is mobile and linked to public spaces'.[6] But these observations, as rooted as they are in both everyday experience and in the oral histories passed down from grandmother to granddaughter, cannot easily be drawn, modelled or rendered visible. Little wonder Lekalakala turned to the Surrealists.

Left: Kgaugelo
Lekalakala, *Tales of the
Vulnerability of African
Women in Transit Spaces,*
2019. Migrate.

Above: Kgaugelo
Lekalakala, *Tales of the
Vulnerability of African
Women in Transit Spaces,*
2019. Passing through the
passage.

Right: Kgaugelo
Lekalakala, *Tales of the
Vulnerability of African
Women in Transit Spaces,*
2019. Floods of tradition.

Gugu Mthembu, *The Port of Sihr*,
2019. Prologue: Scene 1, Aicha
Qandicha of the Military.

In *Playing in the Dark: Whiteness and the Literary Imagination*, 1992, Nobel Laureate Toni Morrison states, 'the kind of work I have always wanted to do requires me to learn how to manoeuvre ways to free up the language from its sometimes sinister, frequently lazy, almost always predictable employment of racially informed and determined chains'.[7] A similar desire to 'free up' architectural language (both drawn and written), persuaded Gugulethu Mthembu and Heidi Lu, both students in Unit 12 run by myself and Sumayya Vally, at the GSA, to turn away from conventional drawings and texts to performance and film, in their attempts to 'give voice and form' to questions of race, identity, hybridity and gender. Gugu Mthembu's work, seen in stills, performance drawings and photographs in this essay, can also be viewed online.[8] Her thesis, entitled *The Port of Sihr*, draws heavily on mythology, oral history and traditional 'women's crafts' – knitting, weaving, crocheting, sewing – to construct a performance which is both a historical reenactment of a centuries-old Arabic myth and a retelling of contemporary, black South African female identity, circumscribed by tradition, religion and the state.

Act 01
Scene 01

Year: 1700s

Many of these women were teenagers (for procreational reasons, the bulk of women were young adults), leaving behind weeping parents, children and lovers, to travel to God only knows where, aboard a creaking, leaking vessel, accompanied by cows they were expected to milk while the waves were as high as mountains (this task was given to cattle thieves) and sailors they were expected to provide with sex.

Year: 1700s

The Floating Brothel is a story of bodies and their waste, expulsion and overflow. It is about the late 18th century's attempt to control what is undesirable and about how those expelled then lived in the company of each other's waste. The story Sian Rees tells is, among other things, a vivid, visceral, and riveting account of noxious stenches. Smells are becoming a respectable part of historical writing: Peter Ackroyd devotes a chapter of London: A Biography to bad odours, and Sian Rees gives us an ark of "dead rats, dead cats, compost of mounds of vegetable peelings, faeces, urine, rotting fabric and decomposing sick".

Act 02
Scene 03

Year: 1950s

For decades Tangier and other Moroccan cities were magnets for gay tourists. Prior to independence in 1956 Tangier was an international zone that was administered by several different European countries, without a very rigid rule of law. In the words of the English academic Andrew Hussey, Tangier was "a utopia of dangerous, unknown pleasures." The Americans who turned up in the 1950s were escaping from a repressive society where homosexuality was outlawed. In Morocco, attitudes were much more relaxed and, provided they were discreet, Westerners could indulge their desires, without fear of harassment, with a limitless supply of young locals in need of money, and smoke an equally limitless supply of the local cannabis.

Gugu Mthembu,
The Port of Sihr,
2019. Act 3, Floating
Brothel Act Timeline.

Act 02
Scene 03
Year:

The Courtyard"
During the Ottoman empire, many women's
interactions were limited to socialization's
among fellow women, and members of their
family. Women socialized with each other at
their homes and also at bathhouses. High
society women, particularly those who did not
live in the palace, visited one another at each
other's homes. Those who lived in the palace
were subject to strict etiquette that prevented
ease of socializing

Act 02
Scene 01
Year:

Women's Door
The concubines were guarded by enslaved eunuchs,
themselves often from pagan Africa. The eunuchs were
headed by the Kizlar Agha ("agha of the [slave] girls").
While Islamic law forbade the emasculation of a man,
Ethiopian Christians had no such compunctions; thus,
they enslaved and emasculated members of territories to
the south and sold the resulting eunuchs to the
Ottoman Porte.

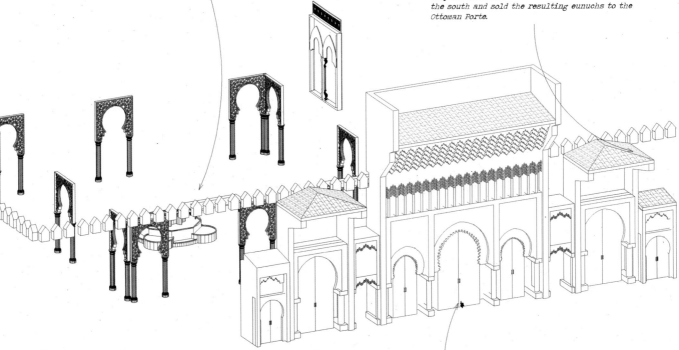

Act 02
Scene 02
Year:

"Legal Mother"
The mother of a new sultan came to the harem with pomp, circumstance and assumed
the title of valide sultan or sultana mother upon her son's ascension. She was
paramount chief and ran the Harem and ruled over the members of the dynasty. The
Valide Sultan who influenced the political life of the Ottoman Empire during
various periods of history (such as the Sultanate of Women in the 16th and 17th
centuries) had the authority to regulate the relations between the sultan and his
wives and children. At times the valide sultan acted as regent for her son,
particularly in the seventeenth century, when a series of accidents necessitated
regencies that endowed the position of Queen Mother with great political power

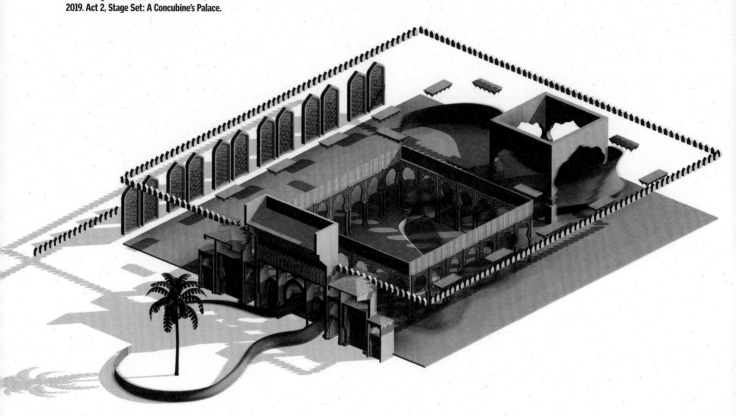

In Mthembu's work, which is also underpinned by a desire to explore black female identity and subjectivity, rather than address (or confront) issues directly, through the lens of her own experience and history, she does so through the history of an 'other', Aicha Qandicha, a Moroccan folkloric, shapeshifting female spirit who appears primarily in men's dreams, enticing them to commit the three, great male 'sins': impotency, infidelity and homosexuality. Seen as a seductress, well-versed in feminine wiles, Aicha Qandicha nevertheless absolves men of the responsibility of their actions – as Mthembu has noted, 'the boy just can't help it'.[9] Through her careful linguistic and etymological analyses, Mthembu draws on unexpected links and relationships between words, myth and meaning to establish a counter-narrative for both Aicha Qandicha and herself (Mthembu). As she notes, 'the word رحس (*sihr*) in Arabic means both "glamour" and "magic". Interestingly, in English, the word *glamour* comes from the Welsh *grameyre*, which is also the word for magic, or illusion. Illusion and veiling are at the core of the word glamour, implying that there are tactics of deceit, concealment, power and mystery at the heart of what it is to be "glamorous", always already gendered.'[10] Mthembu's project, *The Port of* رحس is located between two myths: the mythical figure of Aicha Qandicha and the myth of the feminine. Her 'new' story places Aicha Qandicha in three different 'sites', repatriating her from a concubine slave ship to the Moroccan civil Courts of Law and finally, the King's Palace. Using the 'mashrabiya', a projecting oriel window enclosed with carved wood latticework that is characteristic of Arabic architecture and was historically used to shield women in the home or harem from the prying eyes of men, she proposes a number of new, reconfigured mashrabiya that play with the strict Islamic and Arabic codes of feminine identity through new architectural devices that veil, shade, shield and expose in different ways.

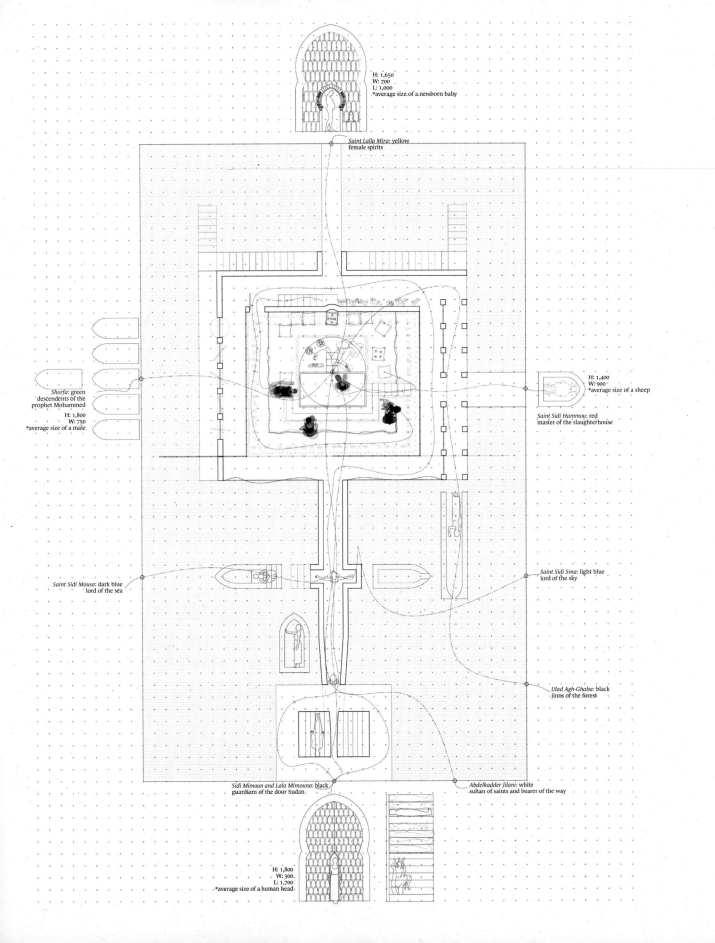

H: 1,650
W: 700
L: 1,000
*average size of a newborn baby

Saint Lalla Mira: yellow
female spirits

Shorfa: green
descendents of the
prophet Mohammed
H: 1,800
W: 750
*average size of a male

H: 1,400
W: 900
*average size of a sheep

Saint Sidi Hammou: red
master of the slaughterhouse

Saint Sidi Mousa: dark blue
lord of the sea

Saint Sidi Sma: light blue
lord of the sky

Ulad Agh-Ghaba: black
jinns of the forest

Sidi Mimoun and Lala Mimouna: black
guardians of the door Sudan.

Abdelkadder Jilani: white
sultan of saints and bearer of the way

H: 1,800
W: 300.
L: 1,700
*average size of a human head

In Heidi Lu's hands, history is malleable and material, a means not to understand the world 'as it was', but rather 'what it could or should have been'. In her thesis project, *Casablanca: The Port of Homes*, her investigations into the spatial, formal and material languages of the binary pairing 'home/diaspora' encompass dance, sculpture, song, film and site-specific installations. Moving from the first home of the body (pregnancy) to the final home of history (a repository where the stories we tell ourselves about ourselves are laid, allegorically speaking, to rest), she is as comfortable making as she is in orthographic projection and performance. Over the course of two years in Unit 12, as she grew in confidence and range, her work shifted from the intimate and somewhat self-conscious scale of her own body and history to a much broader and wider understanding of 'belonging' as a necessary condition for an authentic architectural culture to take root.

Above: Heidi Lu, *Casablanca: The Port of Homes*, 2019. Look into My Eyes, One Last Time.

Right: Heidi Lu, *Casablanca: The Port of Homes*, 2019. Right Foot Step Right, Left Foot Tap Right.

Left: Heidi Lu, *Casablanca: The Port of Homes*, 2019. Lila.

Street colloquium and
exhibition convened by Dr
Huda Tayob and curated by
Counterspace, GSA, University
of Johannesburg, 2019.
Photograph, Sumayya Vally.

Part 3
Dark Matters

It is important to note that all three projects were protected by the explicitly decolonising project of the school as a whole. From the moment of its inception in 2014, the GSA's agenda has always been to provide a safe space for students to simultaneously explain and explore their own histories and identities through the lens and means of architectural education. Founded against the backdrop of unfolding student protests in 2015 and 2016, staff and students were collectively able to embrace risk and curriculum innovation in ways that would have been challenging in more conservative times and climes. With the larger project of 'history' at stake, particularly in South Africa, the cultural and political ambivalence regarding the 'truth' of history was opportune. In the post-colony, history is always contested. Whose history? Told from whose perspective? At whose expense? Nearly 60 years ago, the British historian Hugh Trevor-Roper declared, 'Perhaps in the future there will be some African history to teach. But at present there is none; only the history of Europeans in Africa. The rest is darkness; the unedifying gyrations of barbarous tribes in picturesque but irrelevant corners of the globe. And darkness is not the subject of history'.[11] The opening provided by the protests afforded participants at the school, (whether tutors or students) to robustly answer Trevor-Roper's charge in the most effective way possible – by and through design. In contrast to many other places where attempts to make curricular or programmatic changes can take months, if not years, to achieve, the political climate enabled the school to take much more radical and experimental risks almost immediately. The design studio was 'opened up' to take in history and theory by collapsing two modules and taking – quite literally – seminars into the streets. As the South African Council for the Architectural Profession (SACAP) noted during its five-year accreditation visit to the GSA in 2018:

The proportion of black students within the GSA is notable as amongst the highest of any Master's programme in South Africa. It is evident that one of the key successes of the application of the Unit System has been the creation of space for black students to find their voice and express their architectural identity through their research and design work, an important step against the backdrop of the agenda for the decolonisation of higher education.

It is commonly understood that the depth and degree to which history was subverted in South Africa in order to control and exploit the existing, indigenous population has no parallels anywhere else on the African continent. Settler societies are almost unique in their ability and mandate to erase, overwrite and overrule. However, in the same way that history can never be completely or fully erased, no matter how biased or unreliable, resistance and rebellion too are remarkably tenacious. Lekalakala, Mthembu and Lu are all shaped by the history of apartheid but, through their work, are also free of it. The space of the design studio or project may not yet be a literal, material and tactile space but it has allowed all three to claim their own space within the confines of architectural language, which is every much a part of the decolonising process as bricks and mortar. As the Kenyan writer Mũkoma wa Ngũgĩ writes, 'language carries the entire body of values by which we come to perceive ourselves and our place in the world'.[12]

Verwoerd is turning in his grave.

1 From a private email correspondence following the nationwide Black Lives Matter protests, May 2020..
2 D. F. Malan, House of Assembly Debates (HAD), 1944, col. 75, quoted in Hermann Giliomee, 'The Making of the Apartheid Plan, 1929–1948', *Journal of South African Studies*, vol 29, issue 2, June 2003, p 374.
3 Deborah Posel, *The Making of Apartheid, 1948–1961: Conflict and Compromise*, Oxford, Clarendon Press, 1991, p 297.
4 Kgaugelo Lekalakala, 'Tales of the Vulnerability of African Black Women in Transit Spaces', *City*, vol 24, issue 1–2, 2020, pp 233–243.
5 Ibid., pp 233–243.
6 Ibid., pp 233–243.
7 Toni Morrison, *Playing in the Dark: Whiteness and the Literary Imagination*. Cambridge MA and London, Harvard University Press, 1992, p xii

8 UJ GSA, 'Gender & Architecture 04', *Vimeo*, https://vimeo.com/393024444, 2020, (accessed 12 February 2021).
9 From tutorial conversations with Gugu Mthembu, Unit 12, GSA, 2019.
10 Gugu Mthembu, The Port of ر حس Major Design Project, Unit 12, Graduate School of Architecture, University of Johannesburg, 2019. Supervised by Sumayya Vally.
11 The statement was originally made during a series of lectures in the University of Sussex transmitted by BBC Television. The lectures appeared in print in *The Listener* in 1963 and finally became a book: Hugh Trevor-Roper, *The Rise of Christian Europe*, London, Harcourt, Brace & World, 1965, pp 9–11.
12 Mũkoma wa Ngũgĩ, 'What Decolonizing the Mind Means Today', https://lithub.com/mukoma-wa-ngugi-what-decolonizing-the-mind-means-today/, 23 March 2020 (accessed 14 August 2020).

Níall McLaughlin and
Yeoryia Manolopoulou

Drawing Together

We taught Unit 17 at The Bartlett School of Architecture at University College London between 1999 and 2019. Typically, a group of about 16 students spent two years together. In 2018, we travelled to Orkney with one group and they made a collective drawing. We suggest that the way in which the students used the emerging drawing to create a world with its own internal coherence has certain parallels with Neolithic settlers on the islands, harnessing collaborative activity to bind a community in a place. From this, it is possible to argue an understanding of architecture as an embodiment of communal processes. These are subject to endless renewal and are therefore inherently unfinishable.

Orkney is a collection of islands off the north coast of Scotland. Our group explored the archipelago for five days. We walked across the islands every day and the students made one large drawing together in the evenings. We hoped each activity would inform the other, but we were not explicit about how that might happen. The group assembled at dusk in a hall tucked behind the twelfth-century CE St Magnus Cathedral in Kirkwall. They drew until midnight. We expected that a dialogue would emerge naturally between their growing understanding of the landscape and the way in which the drawing came about. We decided not to discuss this verbally, but to allow matters to rise to their attention through working quietly as an ensemble.

Islands

The Orkney archipelago was created by an infinitely gradual, falling drift of sand: wash over wash of fine-grained particles laid gently on an older geological surface and then compacted by subsequent layers pressing down on top. It formed a stratified crust of Old Red Sandstone on a metamorphic basement.[1] The nature of the stone varies depending on the mode of deposition. There are characteristic patterns resulting from how the grains were laid down, either by shifting wind or in the slow stillness of lakes. Moving streams spread their conical fans of alluvial sediment, poured out in a wavering, cyclical process. Occasionally, marine incursions spilt their disruptions into the many layers. As the sediments deepened and were subjected to pressure, they fractured into flagstones. The scribbled calligraphy of stress is written everywhere in tiny cracks and fissures. Periodically, the earth tilted slightly on its axis, turning away from the sun, and glaciers returned. Massive bergs of ice, half a kilometre-deep, scoured and gouged the stone surface. Then they retreated, laying new material

in their wake in mounds and banks of glacial till. Marking, erasing, repeating.

This cluster of islands is caught in a continuous dance with the sea. As the great weight of ice melted after the last Ice Age, the water level began to rise. At the same time, the earth, relieved of its burden, rebounded upwards. The land and sea rose simultaneously, but not at the same speed. The relative change in sea level produced different phenomena in different places. There are raised beaches eight metres above sea level and there are drowned forests where the water has inundated old wooded landscapes.[2] Even now, this ballet is active, as the rising tide tears at the land and exposes hidden histories. Recently, at Cata Sand in Sanday, a dune was ripped away by waves in a storm, revealing a Neolithic house underneath.[3] The next storm might strip away the whole house and take it into the depths. This world is emerging and dissolving all at once.

Once the ice retreated, a newly exposed surface was colonised by plants and creatures migrating upriver against chaotic streams of glacial outwash. Human hunters followed them. These people found an environment of great variety, including sheer cliffs, sandy bays, salt marshes, oak forest, carr woodland and upland pasture. At the boundaries between these conditions, known as ecotones, there were opportunities for a large range of living species capable of providing nutrition for small mobile communities. People wandered through different landscapes on a seasonal basis, changing their diet as each new situation afforded, allowing the earth to replenish itself in the areas they left behind.[4] They lived so lightly that their trajectories, tools, constructions and beliefs have now almost vanished. Only if you pay close attention to the hidden manuscript of the land, can you perceive the petrified echo of one of their activities: tool making. Here and there, like rain dropping into a still pool, you find concentric circles of flint fragments scattered around a lost hearth. Each broken-off shard is a sounding, pointing back to the repetitive percussion of flint knapping.[5] If you strain to the limit, you might intuit the social structure of these groups from the relative disposition of scatterings. The flecks of discarded material in the circles are not always evenly distributed. In some places, the fragments have been struck off in a neat and expert way, in others they are slightly clumsy.[6] This speaks of working groups clustered by age and experience, teaching and learning in an apprenticeship to a lifelong skill.

Agriculture marked the archipelago more than any other human process. Today, the landscape is a stratigraphy of organised production laid down in different eras. It is inscribed with enclosures, old turf cuttings, hill dykes, midden pockets, drains, quarries, the ghosts of walls and a lost labyrinth of runrig cultivation strips.[7] Ploughing, draining and scattering were agents of continuous transformation. Significant buildings were situated at boundaries: the houses clustered between field and shore, the tombs on higher ground between cultivated land and upland pasture. They were always at the edge, constantly visible.[8]

Not all vectors are cut physically into the land. Invisible forces act in constant procession. Overwhelming tidal currents surge between shores. There is an endless store of words for wind: *kuil, tirl, gurl, skuther, skolder* and *screevar*.[9] Every projecting form has its lee, a wind-shadow world of congregation and production. Today, islanders imagine a future made prosperous by harnessing wind and tidal forces to generate electricity.

The sea roads carried ideas from beyond the horizon, motifs were transplanted from Avebury, the Boyne and Scandinavia. Above the constant rhythm of the seasons and the sea, cultures came and went. Picts were replaced by Vikings, who eventually ceded the islands to Scotland in the fourteenth century. The great clearances of the eighteenth century profoundly changed the population and their ownership of the land. Huge drainage projects opened up new farmland while the old runrig land patterns disappeared beneath the visible horizon. Orkney fishing towns became central to the North Atlantic and Arctic whaling industries. If you were sailing far north, you collected your crew at Stromness.

Drawing

Our group arrived into Stromness by ferry on a winter night. We stayed together in a hotel on the waterfront in Kirkwall. From there, it was a short walk to our hall behind the cathedral. It had a high-pitched roof and was overlooked by a little mezzanine from which you could see the emerging drawing laid out on the floor. Next to the hall, there was another room with a long table where we could eat together and rest. We worked on the drawing in the evenings when it was dark outside and we could not see out, giving an inward quality to the experience.

In the short daylight hours, we travelled the islands by car, boat and on foot. Wherever possible, we walked. We took a ferry across the great natural harbour of Scapa Flow at dawn, sounding down in our imaginations to the sunken fleet of battleships that lay just beneath. We climbed the Old Man of Hoy and

gazed back across the water to the Neolithic monuments around the Ring of Brodgar. We lay in silence on the floor of Olav's Wood, listening to the Atlantic gales heaving through the trees overhead. At low tide, we crossed a fragile causeway onto the Viking ruins at the Brough of Birsay, dashing back just in time as the racing tide rose rapidly around our feet. We stood on an exposed strand, our voices drowned out by the roar of the surf. We dropped down into the corbelled cores of old tombs, where the sudden silence was as pressing as the darkness around us. When we walked, we fell into step in little groups allowing intimate conversations, discovering more about each other as we made our way.

On the first evening, we laid out a field of white paper. We sat around the edge and discussed how we might proceed. It was important to initiate a process without determining any sense of a finished form. The role of the teachers was not to draw or to direct the drawing. Our task was to instigate the event and to pay attention as it unfolded. We wandered around amongst the drafters, discussing the relationship between the making of a drawing and the making of a place. We wanted to allow the drawing to emerge as spontaneously as possible from the condition that we found ourselves in. We decided that the size of the drawing could be determined by allowing everyone to lie in a circle on the floor with arms stretched out in front so that all of their fingertips were just touching. As they withdrew their hands and arms, a white expanse opened up from the tips of their fingers to the tips of their toes. In this way, the space of the drawing was given by the volume and reach of their bodies. The drafters occupied this space in little clusters and, as they began to draw, the areas between each group were filled with lines and the places where they sat or knelt at work were left white and unmarked. The boundaries between inscribed and empty space constantly shifted as groups moved about and individuals ferried between clusters.

The participants never instructed or corrected one another. They worked into and around each other's marks without judgement: looking for opportunities, disjunctions or harmonies. They made no attempt to depict, record or represent an external reality. Roles were not allocated to individuals. The act of drawing as a community made its own horizon. New modes of invention and communication emerged out of the growing presence of the drawing itself. Organised uncertainty prevailed, in which individual autonomy found a delicate balance with collaboration, each extending the possibilities of the other. It was not a predictable process, but, as it went on, a coherence emerged. Mutual recognition came about through ways and methods, rather than through a focus on ends. The work was not so much foreseen as continually inhabited. As a social artefact, it was inherently unfinishable.

The paper was a thick white cartridge brought in 3ft wide rolls. It was laid out in strips that were closely butt jointed. The edges were fixed to the floor with a continuous perimeter of masking tape. We chose to begin drawing with fine black ink pens, partly because we wanted one point of common identity at the outset using commonplace tools, but also since this single material had a correlation to the unified persistence of stone material culture on the islands. At the start, students brought formal drafting tools with them from the studio: pens, compasses, rulers and French curves. As the process went on, these were augmented with found instruments from the landscape. Round beach pebbles dipped in ink were rolled across the surface; flat sandstone wafers were sharpened into palette knives and used to scrape and smear; seashells were adapted as fragile ink pots. Individuals and groups developed novel techniques of delineation, hatching, printing, scratching, erasing and embossing and they shared them in a way that was both competitive and cooperative. A line of sewing thread held people's hands together as they drew. When it was discarded, it lay in long loops across the expanse of paper for an instant before it was brushed away.

In practice, the ongoing event was often reminiscent of the parlour game Twister, where players have to find ways to accommodate increasingly contorted combinations of bodies on a small mat. The limited space of the drawing required individuals and groups to work around each other in close, often elaborately proximate contact. These cosy physical accommodations heightened the sense of intimacy within the group and we noticed a deepening connection between the participants as the days wore on. The expanse of the drawing, the ordinary available tools and the bodies of the participants made an environment from which new possibilities for action naturally emerged.

The drawing had its own time signature that was linked to the rhythms of the day and the wider landscape. It was part of a set of interlinked, repetitive rituals: waking, dining, hiking, picnicking, returning, rolling out the drawing, reflecting, drawing, drinking and sleeping. The extension out towards the broad horizon of the islands each morning was balanced by a contraction back to the hall in the evening, before a further expansion into the space of the drawing. Each time we returned to it, the group had been changed and so had the drawing. The collaborators were shaping the piece and being shaped by it. The cyclical nature of this flow and return process was not only central to the work, but also to its relation to the social and physical processes that had created both the environment and culture of the islands. It allowed us to think of the world not as determined form, but as an overlapping set of reciprocal processes that could only be understood in time. Considered in this way, time unpicks the knot of authorship, opening the work to multiple intentions, insights and contributions. It is not simply that the group is there to create the work; at a deeper level, the work is a way of creating the group.

Building

The first settlers on these islands came by sea. Their world lay between the landscape of the archipelago and the tools and memories they brought with them. Their buildings acted primarily as a locus for family groups and communities who moved around the land.[10] It can be argued that the original purpose of houses was to extend the social connections between individuals in time.[11] Building and telling stories expanded the temporal horizon of mobile groups and alleviated the stresses generated by increasingly complex social structures. Within this understanding, the house was not a finite artefact, but a long process involving initiation, transformation, demolition and recreation, ultimately following the emergence and passing of human generations.[12] Houses may have been understood like human bodies in their cycles of renewal, decay and memorial. As such, they acted as a conduit through which known and hidden things passed. A home could equally be understood as a structure, a body and a model of the cosmos.[13]

As the Neolithic transformation passed through the archipelago, tombs, standing stones and stone circles were built from increasingly durable materials. The stone was taken from the beautifully fractured stacks of sandstone flags and laid in patterns that seem to imitate its stratified and folded lineaments. We can see evidence of wedging, splitting and lifting rocks from their geological beds.[14] The stones often hold inscriptions on their concealed faces, marking transitions and thresholds: parallel lines, chevrons, zig zags and crosshatching are cut into their surfaces.[15] They are like hidden re-inscriptions of those old faults we find in the rock itself.

There is some evidence that oak once grew on the islands. The first houses were probably communal structures made from wood and wattle.[16] They are lost to us now, but sometimes we find regular punctuation marks in the earth marking postholes.[17] We know nothing else. We learn most about the living from the shadow cast by them onto the tombs of the dead. Linear stone barrows, divided into stalls, are probably skeuomorphs of wooden long houses.[18] It is likely that these houses predated and participated in the gradual thickening of human communities into forms of settled life. Accumulated material possessions slowed down these mobile communities and bound them more tightly into fixed places on the earth.[19] The sophisticated invisible network of kinship and affiliation between endlessly moving groups gradually ossified into permanent forms in the land. The use of stone in their tombs may have instigated greater investment into a durable relationship with particular places, one that superseded any single generation. To lay claim to your own piece of land, you need a history.

In a beautiful reversal, new masonry houses were created in imitation of stone tombs. Homes became history houses.[20] They were built and rebuilt again and again, insistently on their own foundations.[21] To live in a house was to connect the dead to the unborn in a particular place.[22] Some homes have a deep *millefeuille* of burnt charcoal surfaces beneath the hearthstone, witnessing the passing of fire upwards through the layers, as each floor level was rebuilt at the turning of a generation. Precious sheep and cattle skulls were interwoven with the foundations to memorialise communal relationships between families and herds.[23]

While there is some evidence of specialised skills involved in construction, it is accepted that building was carried out by extended communities during gaps in the agricultural cycle.[24] This was accompanied by feasting and the ritual interment of fragments of human and animal remains. The process of construction and the duration of use were closely linked to the passing of generations. The open-ended nature of this process points to a role for the activity itself as being central to the internal cohesion of larger social groups. For a house, this might be an extended family, for a tomb it might be neighbours sharing a stretch of shore; but the great stone circles at Stenness and Brodgar provide evidence of material brought from the wider archipelago.[25] The assembly of these monuments seemed to involve widely dispersed communities coming to a central place with their families and their herds; bringing great stones dragged across the land for incorporation into a binding arrangement.

Such alliances were strategic, fault lines could open between households as the heads of families sought to assert their influence. One way to reduce that risk was to use the act of building as an equivalent for blood, as a way of making others show their commitment to the community through residence and involvement in the architectural process.[26]

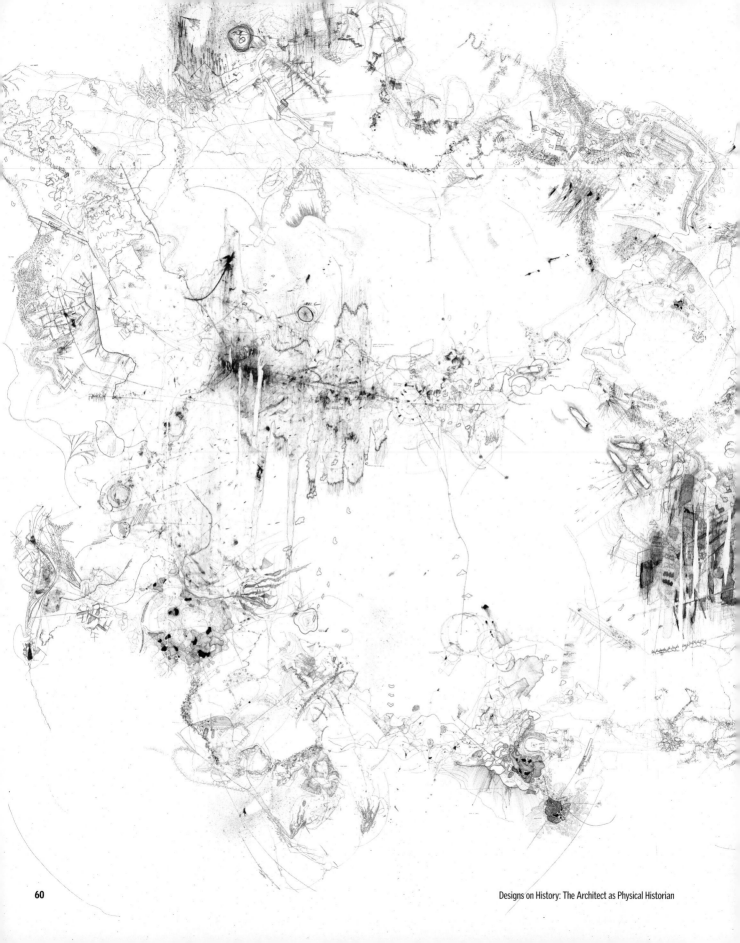

Designs on History: The Architect as Physical Historian

Recent work on the Ring of Brodgar points to it as a place of cyclical ritual assembly. The Ring is positioned at a key transition in a wider landscape, linked visually to other significant monuments at the centre of the archipelago. It has been suggested that its geometry may relate to solar and lunar alignments.[27] Inspection of its foundations shows that the Ring was never completed and, indeed, the foundation sockets were not built for permanence.[28] It is tantalising to think that its long duration is an accident of its material properties and that, in fact, it was always a provisional arrangement. It might be only one cut from an ongoing process of transformation and rearrangement. If we accept this idea, the architecture was not an assembly of objects but an ongoing performance. Widely dispersed communities would bring their tired bodies together to bind these stones into a ring, containing a space in the landscape, renewing their obligations to each other and opening themselves out to the cosmos.

The dominant architectural culture of our own time remains focused on the authorship of visually sensational artefacts. Each has a perfect moment of conception predicated on individual subjectivity and everything thereafter – construction, weathering, use and alteration – puts this idealised identity at risk.[29] In this paradigm, drawing is a way of fixing a building at its conception rather than a method of exploring processes of becoming with their own natural duration. By returning to the origins of architecture in Neolithic culture, where it operates as a collective performance, binding communities together in time, we hope to suggest another way of thinking. When our students draw together, they imaginatively rehearse the overlapping processes by which a place and culture come into being. In doing this, they form deep and lasting connections with each other in that place. We hope that this will bind them into their own ring that will support them through their education and into their lives as architects.

Images: Nathan Back-Chamness, Luke Bryant, Eleni Efstathia Eforakopoulou, Ossama Elkholy, Grace Fletcher, George Goldsmith, Kaiser Hud, Hanrui Jiang, Rikard Kahn, Cheuk Ko, Alkisti Anastasia Mikelatou Tselenti, Veljko Mladenovic, Iman Mohd Hadzhalie, Andreas Müllertz, Philip Springall and Harriet Walton with Yeoryia Manolopoulou and Niall McLaughlin, Orkney Drawing, 2018.

1   Walter Mykura, *British Regional Geology: Orkney and Shetland*, Edinburgh, Her Majesty's Stationery Office, 1976, s 1.8.
2   Steven Mithen, *After the Ice: A Global Human History, 20,000–5,000 BC*, London, Weidenfeld & Nicolson, 2003, p 154.
3   University of the Highlands and Islands Archaeology Institute, *Archaeology Orkney*, https://archaeologyorkney.com/category/cata-sand/, (accessed 2 October 2020).
4   Mark Edmonds, *Orcadia: Land, Sea and Stone in Neolithic Orkney*, London, Head of Zeus, 2019, pp 32–35; Mithen, op cit, pp 196–206.
5   Nicholas Crane, *The Making of the British Landscape: From the Ice Age to the Present*, London, Weidenfeld & Nicolson, 2016, p 14.
6   Mithen, op cit, pp 127–128.
7   Edmonds, op cit, pp 9–10.
8   Ibid., pp 87–88.
9   Ibid., p 11.
10 Richard Bradley, *The Prehistory of Britain and Ireland*, Cambridge, Cambridge University Press, 2007, p 59.
11 Ian Hodder, *Two Forms of History Making in the Neolithic of the Middle East, Religion, History and Place in the Origin of Settled Life*, Boulder, University Press of Colorado, 2018, pp 3–10.
12 Ibid., pp 8–9.
13 Trevor Garnham, *Lines on the Landscape, Circles from the Sky: Monuments of Neolithic Orkney*, Stroud, Tempus, 2004, p 45.
14 Edmonds, op cit, p 79.
15 Ibid., pp 259–262.
16 Michelle Farrell, M. Jane Bunting, Daniel H. J. Lee, and Antonia Thomas, 'Neolithic Settlement at the Woodland's Edge: Palynological Data and Timber Architecture in Orkney, Scotland', *Journal of Archaeological Science*, vol 51, November 2014, pp 225–236.
17 Colin Richards and Andrew Merrion Jones, *Houses of the Dead: The Transition from Wood to Stone Architecture at Wideford Hill, The Development of Neolithic House Societies in Orkney*, Oxford, Windgather Press, 2016, pp 16–30.
18 Richard Bradley, *The Prehistory of Britain and Ireland*, Cambridge, Cambridge University Press, 2007, p 86; Luc Laporte and Jean-Yves Tinévez, 'Neolithic Houses and Chambered Tombs of Western France', *Cambridge Archaeological Journal*, vol 14, no 2, October 2004, pp 217–234.
19 Ian Hodder, *Çatalhöyük, The Leopard's Tale*, London, Thames & Hudson, 2006, pp 237–240.
20 Ibid., p 149.
21 Edmonds, op cit, pp. 134, 139.
22 Robert Pogue Harrison, *The Dominion of the Dead*, Chicago, University of Chicago Press, 2003, pp. 39–40.
23 Edmonds, op cit, pp 139–143.
24 Vicki Cummings, *The Neolithic of Britain and Ireland*, London, Routledge, 2017, p.112.
25 Colin Richards, John Brown, Siân Jones, Allan Hall and Tom Muir, 'Monumental Risk: Megalithic Quarrying at Staneyhill and Vestra Fiold, Mainland, Orkney', in Colin Edwards, ed., *Building the Great Stone Circles of the North*, Oxford, Windgather Press, pp 123–127.
26 Edmonds, op cit, p 138.
27 Garnham, op cit, pp 177–182.
28 Jane Downes, Colin Richards, John Brown, A. J. Cresswell, R. Ellen, A. D. Davies, Allan Hall, Robert McCulloch, David C. W. Sanderson and Ian A. Simpson, 'Investigating the Great Ring of Brodgar, Orkney', in Edwards, *Building the Great Stone Circles of the North*, pp 102–104.
29 Marvin Trachtenberg, *Building in Time: From Giotto to Alberti and Modern Oblivion*, New Haven, Yale University Press, 2010, pp 11–23.

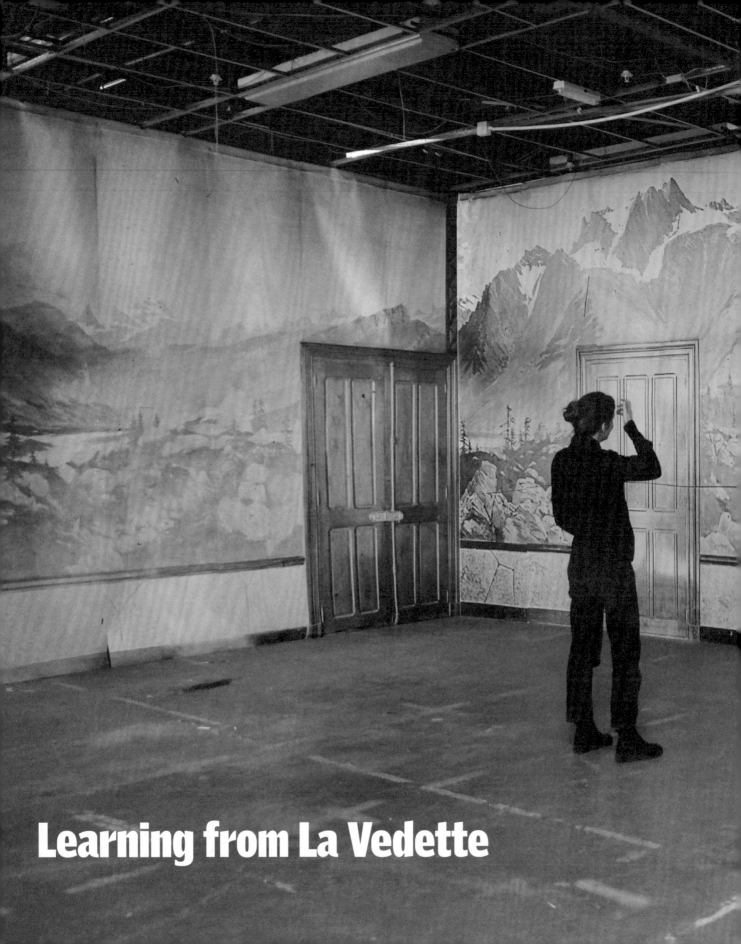

Learning from La Vedette

Reconstructing Viollet-le-Duc's Alpine Study in Lausanne

Aisling M. O'Carroll

Oscillating between the past and present, referent and original, reconstructions are historiographic representations, and yet inevitably also something new. In my design and research practice, I use reconstruction as a methodology that encompasses both historical research and design proposition, offering the opportunity for not only a critical rereading, but also a propositional retelling, of history. In the work presented here, this practice is applied to the retelling of French architect Eugène-Emmanuel Viollet-le-Duc's history through his study of Mont Blanc (1868–1876). His practice is taken as a case study – as both a precedent for the methodology of reconstruction and as the subject of reconstruction itself – in order to critically explore the politics, truth and affective nature of representation in framing knowledge and ideas of landscape.

Viollet-le-Duc's historical investigations were not merely aimed at understanding the past, rather they were intended to provide lessons and knowledge relevant to the present and future. Through careful observation he deduced principles of order that governed the works of Gothic architecture and of nature. He communicated these systems in encyclopaedic detail through lengthy, didactic treatises. And to demonstrate the 'truth' and mastery of his observations, he produced reconstructions not by simply copying what was seen in situ, but by reapplying the systems of order to synthetically produce new typological creations – both architectural and geological. These synthetic reconstructions were achieved by means of his scientific knowledge and artistic skill and realised through drawings, paintings, stories and buildings. However, Viollet-le-Duc's emphasis on rational objectivity obscures his intentional perspective and the ideas embedded within these representations.

His use of representation as a mode of reconstruction reached its ultimate form in his ambitious study of Mont Blanc. Viollet-le-Duc analysed and reconstructed the geological monument through hundreds of drawings, numerous paintings, a map and written treatise on the massif,[1] and an immersive reconstruction in La Vedette, the home he built for himself in Lausanne, Switzerland. As with his other works, these reconstructions were not simply neutral representations of the past but were embedded with the knowledge and ideas that structured his world view and perception of history. By retelling this history, my work illustrates an alternative reading of his reconstructions as ideas that are not universal laws (as he claimed), but rather situated (and limiting) ideas that sprung from his own context, interactions and the circulation of ideas at the time. This reading challenges the dominant narrative of rational objectivity and demonstrates the composite nature of history, opening up space for a critical, and propositional, historiographic practice.

Described as his 'architectural manifesto' by historian Jacques Gubler, La Vedette tied Viollet-le-Duc's ideas of archetypal landscape and architecture together with his world view.[2] Construction of the house began in 1874, on a plot of land purchased on the eastern edge of Lausanne. The home sat on the south-facing slope, looking out over Lake Geneva to the Savoy Alps. It was in the Grande Salle, on the ground floor of the house, that the architect culminated his geological investigation with the installation of a painted panorama depicting a geotectonic reconstruction of the Alpine landscape. The scene spanned the north and west walls of the room. Beyond the landscape's canvas, the architect continued his painterly treatment of the room with painted timber columns, a stone plinth encircling the room and polychromy accents to the ceiling joists. On the south and east walls, half-timbered construction, hanging curtains and climbing plants were painted to complete the scene of an elevated belvedere set within the mountain landscape. As determined by Gubler, the landscape depicted in the panorama was not an existing site. Rather it was an idealised landscape, synthesised through Viollet-le-Duc's geological knowledge.[3] In the folded space of the room, the panorama transformed from individual painted panels to a monumental landscape encircling the architect's dining table, working desk and office.

La Vedette was demolished in 1975, while the
fate of the panorama – which was removed, lost, or
painted over at an earlier point – remains a mystery.
By reconstructing La Vedette and the Grande Salle,
my study retells the story of both the home and the
architect. La Vedette, which has been referred to as
Viollet-le-Duc's 'architectural self-portrait', was more
than a mute container.[4] The home encompassed the
architect's world view and translated it into architectural
form. This investigation of the house reveals the
complexities of his practice, including the slow violence
embedded in his rationalisation of human, architectural
and landscape history.

On one level, La Vedette was a house of love that
Viollet-le-Duc shared with his secretary, Alexandrine
Sureda. While their correspondence has been erased
from the architect's archive, we can speculate about the
intimate nature of their relationship from the records
of the building itself, where the private door conjoining
their two bedrooms is preserved in plans of the first floor.
Mme Sureda's involvement in the Alpine study is also
evident in her appearances in the architect's mountain
sketches and itineraries (she accompanied him on many
of his excursions), as well as in the volumes of recorded
field notes from these excursions, all transcribed in
her handwriting. This female figure, her involvement
in the Alpine study, and their intimate relationship
disrupts the image of the solitary male genius in the
landscape and reframes the architect's investigation
as one that was possibly tempered and qualified by
a second set of eyes and hands. Sureda's handwriting
attests to a circulation of ideas that we can reasonably
assume extended through conversations between the
two in the study and in the field. In addition to Sureda,
several others would likely have shaped the work,
although they are largely left out of accounts, including
the guides Viollet-le-Duc travelled with, locals he met
along the way, and the geologists and naturalists that he
corresponded with. This larger network of individuals

reflects the contingency of the architect's field work and the exchanges that, in addition to his direct observations, helped shape his Alpine investigation.

Simultaneously, the home bears witness to deeply troubling associations of race and nation embedded in the architect's reading of the Alpine landscape. In his architectural novella, *Histoire de l'habitation humaine*, published in 1875, in the midst of his Alpine investigation and construction of La Vedette, Viollet-le-Duc traces an ethnographic and explicitly racial history of the development of vernacular architecture.[5] In this account he ties the Swiss mountain chalet to the primitive Himalayan mountain dwelling, which he attributes to the superior, Aryan race.[6] According to Viollet-le-Duc, the chalets of the Swiss mountains came closest to preserving the primitive Aryan architecture in its original, unchanged form as they were 'built in the same manner by sections of one and the same race separated long ages ago'.[7] La Vedette, with its steeply pitched roof, deep overhangs and cantilevered front balcony clearly referenced the archetypal mountain hut and its origins, as described in his novella. The timber-framed belvedere of the Grande Salle extends this reference further. In making this link, Viollet-le-Duc directly ties the mountain landscape to his archetypal idea of pure, historical origins. Alongside (and entangled with) his ideas of history and nature's rational order, the disturbing implications of his retrogressive ideas of culture, race and national superiority are embedded in the built house and its painted landscape.[8]

My reconstruction is intended not to monumentalise the house, but rather to bring back into a critical conversation the ideas of landscape embedded within his representations. Herein lies the challenge of learning from La Vedette (which mirrors a common challenge inherent to working with history): it entails the uncomfortable task of distinguishing between the productive and deeply disturbing facets of a single history. My work learns from Viollet-le-Duc's practice

The Himalayan dwelling, depiction in Viollet-le-Duc's *Histoire de l'habitation humaine depuis les temps préhistoriques jusqu'à nos jours*, 1875.

of reconstruction through representation while also revealing the violence of the ideas embedded within his representations, offering an alternate reading of the implications of his rational approach to history and architecture.

The histories of the room and architect are retold through a series of speculative reconstructions of the Grande Salle: an unfolded drawing of the room, a speculative map of the panorama and a full-scale installation of the painted panels. The reconstructions take different forms and mediums, each using various digital and analogue tools to manually trace and reconstruct the architectural space and landscape, following Viollet-le-Duc's emphasis on the importance of cognitive engagement in the process of observation and synthesis. By piecing together the remaining, fragmented evidence of the room and resolving the inconsistencies between documents, the drawings restore different histories and readings of the room and panorama. As with any reconstruction, including Viollet-le-Duc's, the work is necessarily speculative as it fills in the gaps of what is left unknown in the remaining material.

First, the arrangement, painterly treatment and furnishings of the Grande Salle are reconstructed in detail, as precisely as possible, through an orthographic drawing. The walls, the recessed eastern bay window and southern French windows, the protruding columns and painted ceiling are unfolded around the room's floor and furnishings. Referred to by Robin Evans as the 'developed surface drawing', this unfolded representation emphasises the interiority of the Grande Salle as a space closer to the elevated Alps than to the foyer beyond its doors.[9] The linework and render quality codes into the drawing the varying levels of knowledge and speculation applied in its construction. Several elements, such as the north and west walls and panorama, are known with relative certainty as they are documented in drawings as well as photographs. Other details, such as the application of colour and the treatment of the south and east walls, are far more speculative as their reconstruction relies on fragments visible at the edges of photographs or on the written description of the room provided by Maurice Ouradou, Viollet-le-Duc's son-in-law.[10] The reconstruction of these less-documented areas draws on material from the architect's Alpine study, sketches and writing to resolve the missing gaps. As a result, these areas offer the opportunity to layer into the reconstruction references to the architect's interpretation and reading of the landscape, offering a richer retelling of the room. The area to the right of the bow window, for example, is described by Ouradou as having 'costumed figures' painted at half-scale alongside the false half-timbered structure.[11] The reconstruction of these unseen figures allows for Arya's character and narrative from *L'habitation humaine* to be more directly introduced within the room's representation.

In a second reconstruction, the landscape of the panorama is projected into three-dimensional space from the perspective of an observer within the room. The resulting topography is rendered as a map, following

Aisling O'Carroll, *The Grande Salle of La Vedette*, 2020. Montage of drawing and models.

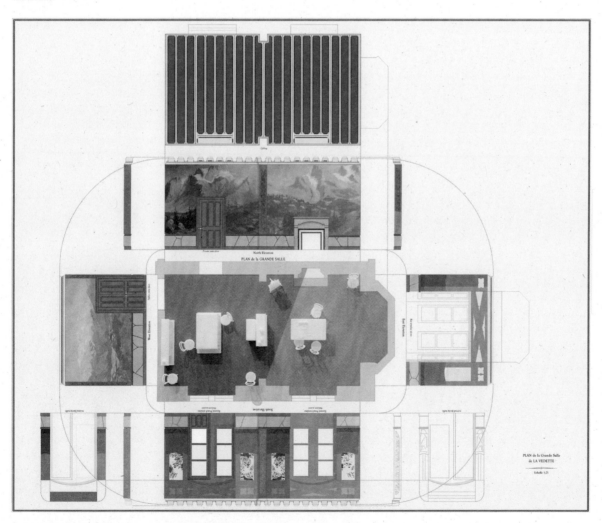

the style of Viollet-le-Duc's map of Mont Blanc. The map offers a view of the landscape not afforded by the panorama and presents it as a navigable and narratable set of places. Through the naming of points, including 'Cime de la Sureda', 'Chutes Gobineau' and 'l'Habitation de l'Hom', layers of Viollet-le-Duc's life at La Vedette and his interpretation of the Alpine landscape are introduced into the panorama. The plotting of trails and routes weaves the connections between these figures and concepts into the topography itself. The map's folds speak to the folds of the room and landscape, while simultaneously folding together the places and names – further overlapping the architect's ideation of landscape, history and architecture through a representation that can be continuously reconfigured.

Finally, a third, immersive reconstruction begins the process of reconstituting the experience of the space – whose immersive, full-scale experience was central to the experience of the reconstructed landscape.

Each of these reconstructions presents a new way of seeing, reading and telling the history of the Grande Salle and Viollet-le-Duc's rationalisation of landscape. The Grande Salle was a model of worldbuilding that demonstrated the architect's power to construct landscape and history through vision (through the panoramic view and its visual representation). By offering new ways of seeing the Grande Salle and its panorama, my series of reconstructions offers alternative ways of organising its world while revealing its underpinnings and limitations. These reconstructions are shaped by Viollet-le-Duc's practice and theory as well as my own knowledge, ideas, methods and tools of representation, producing something new as a result. In this way, the work develops a contemporary practice of design through reconstruction, while simultaneously presenting a critical investigation of historical representations through the work of Viollet-le-Duc, forcing us to question the limitations and inherited ideas in our own ways of seeing and thinking about landscape and architecture.

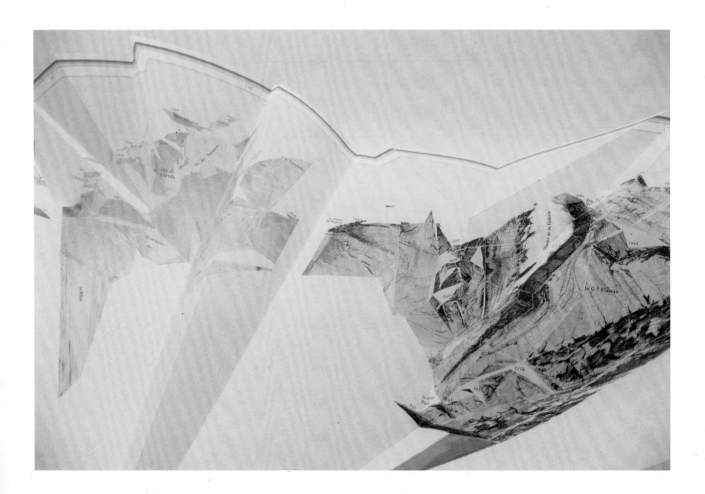

Left and above: Aisling O'Carroll,
Le Massif de La Vedette, carte
dressée à 1:40,000, 2020. Overall
and detail photographs of map.

1   Eugène-Emmanuel Viollet-le-Duc, *Le massif du Mont-Blanc. Étude sur sa construction géodésique et géologique, sur ses transformations, et sur l'état ancien et moderne de ses glaciers*, Paris, Jean Baudry, 1876; Eugène-Emmanuel Viollet-le-Duc, *Le massif du Mont Blanc. Carte dressée à 1 : 40,000, par E. Viollet-le-Duc, d'après ses relevés et études sur le terrain de 1868 à 1875, avec l'aide des minutes du Dépôt Topographique de la Guerre et des levés de M. Mieulet*, 1:40,000, Paris, 1876.
2   Jacques Gubler, 'In Search of the Primitive', in *Eugène-Emmanuel Viollet-le-Duc 1814–1879*, ed. P. Farrant et al., London, Architectural Design and Academy Editions, 1980, p 83.
3   Jacques Gubler, 'Architecture et Géographie: Excursions de lecture ainsi que deux manifestes de Viollet-le-Duc', in *E. Viollet-le-Duc et le massif du Mont-Blanc, 1868–1879*, ed. P. A. Frey, Lausanne, Payot Lausanne, 1988, pp 105–106.
4   Gubler, 'In Search of the Primitive', p 83.
5   Eugène-Emmanuel Viollet-le-Duc, *Histoire de l'habitation humaine depuis les temps préhistoriques jusqu'a nos jours*, Bibliothèque d'éducation et de Récréation, Paris, J. Hetzel, 1875.
6   Viollet-le-Duc's account of the history of vernacular architecture draws heavily on Arthur de Gobineau's *Essai sur l'inégalité des races humaines*, 1853–1855.
7   Eugène-Emmanuel Viollet-le-Duc, *The Habitations of Man in All Ages*, trans. Benjamin Bucknall, Boston, MA, James R. Osgood and Co., 1876, p 384.
8   Laurent Baridon, 'Chalet', in *L'imaginaire scientifique de Viollet-le-Duc, Villes, Histoires, Culture, Société*, Paris, Éditions L'Harmattan, 1996, pp 67–77; Irene Cheng, 'Structural Racism in Modern Architectural Theory', in *Race and Modern Architecture: A Critical History from the Enlightenment to the Present*, ed. Irene Cheng, Charles L. Davis and Mabel O. Wilson, *Culture, Politics, and the Built Environment*, Pittsburgh, PA, University of Pittsburgh Press, 2020, pp 134–51; Charles L. Davis II, 'Campfires in the Salon: Viollet-le-Duc and the Modernization of the Aryan Hut', in *Building Character: The Racial Politics of Modern Architectural Style, Culture, Politics, and the Built Environment*, Pittsburgh, PA: University of Pittsburgh Press, 2020, pp 31–68.
9   Robin Evans, 'The Developed Surface: An Enquiry into the Brief Life of an Eighteenth-Century Drawing Technique', in *Translations from Drawing to Building and Other Essays*, London, Architectural Association, 1997, pp 195–232.
10 Maurice Ouradou, 'La Vedette, maison de Viollet-le-Duc à Lausanne', in *Encyclopédie d'architecture*, vol. X, Paris, A. Morel, 1881, pp 49–51.
11 Ouradou, 'La Vedette, maison de Viollet-le-Duc à Lausanne', p 50.

Above: Pezo von Ellrichshausen, *70611161923*
(Exterior no. 23), oil on canvas, 180 × 240cm, 2016.

Opposite: Pezo von Ellrichshausen, *71809161018*
(Exterior no. 20), oil on canvas, 180 × 240cm, 2016.

Soft Memory

Pezo von Ellrichshausen

Pezo von Ellrichshausen,
Cien House, Concepción,
Chile, 2009–2011.

Under the existential illusion that we could actually step aside from the continuous stream of time in order to look as objectively as possible at the life we are living, we are confronted with an unsolvable tautology. Two early admonitions here. Firstly, we accept the right to avoid solving this contradiction, since there is no possible way out. Secondly, we understand 'the life we are living' with no distinction between labour and leisure, production and contemplation, individual and dual (agreeing that the dual is a sole, discrete, sensitive unit). Of course, this might be read as the romantic licence of a professional and personal partnership, and that is undeniably another fact. All in all, the circular paradox is fairly basic: we have been producing art and architecture not so much as a tool to solve problems but as an intellectual mechanism to propose unprecedented spatial predicaments, to invent open questions, to avoid making 'artistic architecture' and, instead, exploring the manner in which inhabitable objects might be understood as 'architectonic art'. Architectonic or 'the art of constructing systems', following a rather general philosophical connotation, in our view suggests not only the purpose of a single structure, its sense of unity, totality and inner order, but also a kind of reflective attribute. Plainly reflective, like the polished flat surface of a glass, depending on the incidence of light, sometimes invisible, sometimes an opaque mirror, which allows us to look through into an endless landscape while distorting what we are able to see by its own crystalline, fragile, thin thickness. That is, by the material quality of that glass (ranging from a magnifying lens for a microscope or a telescope to a sheer window plane), together with the physical quality of the light that is cast on it (from obscurity to enlightenment to revelation). We have said it a thousand times already, we never use metaphors (not even concepts or diagrams) to refer to the constructions we do, even less so while we are doing them. And yet, the metaphor here seems to be necessary to read the methods and protocols by which those constructions take form. The glass could then be read as a feeble separation, as an invisible limit, a filter from one realm to another. Within the course of time, innocently represented in popular culture as an infinite, uninterrupted line, this filter could be depicted as a perpendicular segment; a more or less short line that one could introduce at any point, at any moment, of that continuous temporal line. This reflecting line, given its transparency, allow for events to flow from one side to the other: from memories to aspirations, from personal recollections or collective archetypes to personal daydreams, ambitions, mimetic desires, impossible paradises and utopias. The insignificance of that perpendicular line, the looking glass, is inversely proportional to the extension of our own intuitions and reason. Thus, the limits of the world do not only reside in the limits of our language, another philosophical enquiry would warn us, but also in the very limitation of our own capacity to project (through language) our current being, our 'living' existence, into the dark domains of infinity, both forwards and backwards. Once more, the metaphor here is instrumental to designate a form of life overlapped with a form of practice and the latter overlapped yet again with a form of understanding 'the art of constructing systems' as the ultimate human endeavour it is. The primary dimension the metaphor illuminates is our fleeting active life in contrast with the

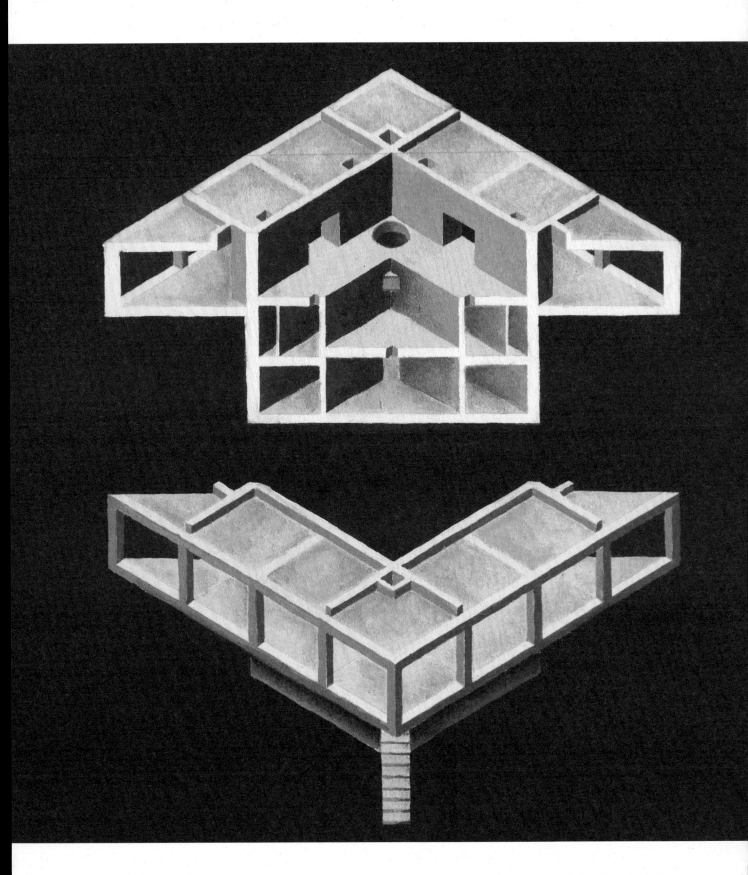

Right: Pezo von
Ellrichshausen, Solo
House, Cretas, Spain,
2009–2013.

Opposite: Pezo von
Ellrichshausen, *Solo*,
axonometric, oil on
canvas, 30 × 30cm, 2013.

overwhelming imaginary history of the known world (devastatingly sublime if one expands it to a universal magnitude). The next metaphoric dimension becomes the explicit illustration of the 'project' that mediates intentionality with the accidental, circumstantial, ever-changing reality of the world, assuming that the project of architecture does not start and does not end with the individual project of a building. A prominent NY architectural prophet defended the opposition between practice and project, between a case overwhelmed by normative constraints and the one that challenges the status quo of the world. A case for sympathetic or ideological architecture which, in our view, further neglects the subjective continuity of one case after another in the author's lifespan while separating the radical from the normal, empathy from abstraction. The third metaphoric dimension, therefore, becomes a form of illusion (or delusion); to be able to find solace in the ethic of productivity, despite its 'useless utility'. The lens of time is a relative mediator. It presents a chain of moments, the instants, as a well-coordinated series of historical events. We collect snapshots of those instants, sometimes we even frame them, we then store them in a special place, thus transfiguring the mundane experience into the sacred representation of that experience. The lens of time alleviates the urgencies of the present. Any memory, a skill, a craft, a technique, becomes a productive tool for works to come. At least conceptually, projects arise from an external prerequisite, from some vacuum or incompleteness that needs to be filled or completed. A family without a house, a collection without a gallery, a production line without a factory, the case itself constitutes the original motivation

for the architectonic intentions to unfold. Nevertheless, the articulation of that particular demand, which in fact can be depicted as a triangular relationship between context, programme and construction, although relevant for the uniqueness of the case, as we see it, is rather irrelevant for the integrity of the work, for its architectonic nature. If not the forces of reality, then what? The inner volition, as many art historians have called it; that energy, the tension, the tendency for something to move in this or that direction. Actually, the problem does not seem to be so much in the existence or not of choice, or the illusion of free will, but in the degree in which that choice becomes open to our consciousness (we like how Bernard Rudofsky labelled the vernacular or 'non-pedigree' architecture as 'unaware of itself').[1] The more education, the more cultivated the human soul, the more aware of everything it produces it should be. And yet, the case is never that linear, never that symmetrical, sometimes even the opposite (Francisco Goya's monsters come to mind). Ignorance can be comprehended as the largest repository of human invention, of imagination and creativity. Beyond the theological implications, we have always been fascinated by the irresponsible resolution by which German mystical-philosopher (and astronomer) Nicholas of Cusa formulated his *De Docta Ignorantia* ('On Learned Ignorance') 1440.[2] If our representational lens allows us to look back and forth in time, ignorance refers to the inexperienced, to that state of mind and body before an actual experience is performed. Ignorance, the lack of knowledge, if we direct it to a positive realm, becomes the ultimate source of original departure for any creative process. An origin that not only implies a primitive,

innate condition but also a non-prejudiced one. Even if
this fiction is a romantic one (we have already uncovered
our warnings), it is not so far from the fairy tales that our
canonised heroes employed as introductions to their own
treatises (from Vitruvius to Laugier, from Viollet-le-Duc
to Van der Laan). The myth of origin, of the first human
inhabitation, of the necessity for shelter, for a
rudimentary obstruction of the natural elements,
confirms the tempting imposition (and also the anxiety)
of a broad unifying architectonic principle. The
validation mechanism, instrumental for the development
of every one of those personal projects, is certainly the
fiction itself: the author-architect is transfigured into an
author-narrator of the rules, methods and techniques
that validate their own practice. Accordingly, the historic
lens, perhaps blurred by emotional disbeliefs, predicts a
certain stream of consequences and effects. Learning,
education and knowledge are founded in this mimetic
practice, in looking for examples, for references, for
steady points where to stand and communicate with
others. History as precedent (the basilica type for
instance) constitutes the model, the ideal example, that is
meant to be imitated (in fact, the basilica plan functions
as a triple imitation; from god to the human body, from
this representation to a geometrical model and from this
figure to the many cases). Hence, the convention
establishes a linear path that connects the model with its
reproduction, or re-creation in the best of cases. The
architect, as the educated animal they are (at least after
the formal training of the last couple of centuries), is
capable of referring back to those lessons from the past
in order to anticipate their effects in the near future.
Architecture, under that model, turns into a form of

eternal return, of moving forward while looking
backward (in a reversed progression, like in the figure
Jefferson-Palladio-Vitruvius). Imitation as such, refers to
a form of anticipation of the unknown by reiterating,
perhaps as a means of consolation or mere self-
protection (or self-preservation), the successful answers
given in the past. This impossible projection (into the
invisible future) is in fact the same for sophisticated and
popular architecture, the academic and the one made by
non-architects. The act of imagining a potential future
reality, the limited means to properly describe it
beforehand, the precise impact it will have over the
natural and cultural landscape that it will occupy, is
transversely cloudy, as inevitably fuzzy as the Platonic
projection out of the cave.[3] The professional, despite his
technological machinery, goes back to the history books
as much as the carpenter to the traditional craft. There is
a kind of natural continuity, conservation and selection,
and the illusion of evolution. In that derivative flow, both
ideal and practical knowledge operate as prejudices that
prejudge the integrity of the new exertions. From our
detached point of view, schematic as it is, there is no
need for formal perfection in order to fulfil a perfect
idea. The Spanish grid system to colonise the 'new world'
is a superb demonstration that we have always been
fascinated with. We understand this ubiquitous urban
form as a 'perfect machine'; an anticipation tool that, in
its own imperfection, erodes any possibility of failure.
The grid as such, as a conquering device, not only
anticipates any possible deviation (mainly
topographical), by imposing a simple geometrical rule,
but also exposes the pathologic fears of the military
enterprise. The formal rule, perfect in its adaptability to

the unknown, was in fact the expression of a terrifying *horror vacui* (perhaps that tender emptiness connects art and war under Minerva's patronage). The implementation of that simple rule, together with the limited skills of the soldiers to interpret a changing dimensional reference (the imprecise *vara* or rod), resulted in a diverse range of urban structures and densities, each one at once unique and the same as the others. Translated into an architectonic scale, a perfect machine would be, for instance, equivalent to the implementation of a non-directional opening (a basic 1:1 ratio aperture) that can be unreservedly articulated on the opacity of a wall. A basic form that admits any size, any function (access, light, ventilation, view, etc.) and any position within the wall. We must admit that these kinds of considerations kept us awake during the first years of our practice. Without knowing it then, we were intrigued by the possibility of referring all formal decisions to anything other than the spatial relationships that would follow the fitting exercise of the case (that triangular articulation we mentioned before). Over the years, we have not only been loyal to that naive intuition but have also understood that the method became a shortcut for us to proceed, to solve architectonic problems, almost without effort. Inexorably, being loyal to a personal modus operandi, similar to personal calligraphy, to handwriting (which one cannot fake when writing in a rush), leads to the mechanical insistence, to the reiterations, the tedious movements over the same principles, over and over again, as in a ritual, becoming a habit. Running in circles, one of us following (or escaping from) the other, up to the point that our steps erode the

grass of the garden and our movement becomes a thick drawing, a leftover of previous steps, which we can no longer differentiate nor avoid. We have realised that our initial method became both a confirmation of our lack of historic references in the development of new ideas and an empirical demonstration of what we later have defined as a self-referential process, of a form that ultimately cannot be the representation of anything because it only refers to itself. The act of running in circles implies the acceptance of an imaginary centre. It also implies the respect for a gravitational trajectory, in the direction of 'the other', at a steady, comfortable distance, while avoiding panoramic distractions, the 360-degree open view to the world. The line, in its rambling contour, becomes a trace of an intimate experience. The original motivation becomes inertia, acceleration and pace. Every turn, each one of us at a different moment, implies a fictional return to the departure point, to a passive beginning. Translated into the practice of architecture, this movement signifies a kind of deceptive attempt to surpass the non-referential by means of the self-referential. The empty circle is the air through which one sees the other. The more distance to the centre, the more ambitious the size of that interior. And yet, there is a point in which the distance is such that it cancels the perception of the other's gestures and expressions (which is precisely what large corporate practices need in order to perform efficiently). Retrospectively, what this circular performance has taught us is twofold. On the one hand, it refers to the concentric effort by which we move from one case to another, to the tediousness of the transitions, to the

Right: Pezo von Ellrichshausen, Nida House, Navidad, Chile, 2014–2016.

Opposite: Pezo von Ellrichshausen, *Nida*, axonometric, oil on canvas, 30 × 30cm, 2015.

Designs on History: The Architect as Physical Historian

slowness of the journey, to the almost theatrical acceptance of invention without any other history than the intimate one (perhaps, as Jorge Luis Borges said,[4] under the belief that one is choosing what is in fact imposed on us, in this case a culture with short memory or no memory at all). As much as the circular movement evidences the very mimetic ethos of our reciprocal practice, doing 'always the same thing but never in the same way' as a poet once advised us, it also epitomises a constant return to an origin, at least to the encouraging delusion of an innate state of mind, a primitive and rather pre-historical understanding of space. Likewise, this circular movement refers to our eager resolution to replace the notion of form by the notion of format. Another semantic deviance that transcends the mere tautology. A format, as we have implemented it, is a substantial formal tendency, a characteristic spatial outline, a continuous silhouette (perhaps a shadow), that determines a certain volume, a field of action for the spatial relationships to unfold. The format, the outline of the architectonic object, is fundamentally spatial since it is determined by two main three-dimensional factors: size and direction. In comparative terms, despite the infinite dimensions a room could have, within a closed system (the architectonic integrity is a conclusive totality) there are only relative sizes. A room could be equivalent to, bigger or smaller than the room next to it. Thus, the format could be reduced to three archetypical sizes: small, medium and large. In the same fashion, direction simply follows the most rudimentary description of space, illustrated with three directions (x, y, z). Accepting this oversimplified formal system,

we have discovered that there are five (only five!) typical architectonic formats derived from a rectangular volume (the most pervasive regular form that unites high and low cultures from different times and places). The cube, the plate, the strip, the bar and the tower, the five basic formats for an orthogonal building, derive from a logic transformation of the three dimensions according to the three sizes).[5] The mechanics of transformations, as much as the spatial structure that every figure contains, become architectural (and not purely geometric or sculptural) insofar as they refer to a supporting base, to a ground (architecture cannot float in the air); thus the radical distinction between a bar and a tower. A linear volume would be insufficient to depict architecture if there is no indication of a potential human scale. This is the function of a rectangular opening (a basic 1:2 ratio) that is intuitively perceived as a door, as a threshold with a size resembling the human body. We have explored these sequences in a large number of paintings, a series we entitled *Finite Format*, alluding to the prescribed finitude, of the prediction, of a limited amount of discrete cases.[6] We believe our buildings have had a similar fate. Within the open, unpredictable formats, and limited set of formal constraints, of internal normative obstructions, the cases have been extended from one to the other, projected as mist, perhaps the smoke of a fire one cannot extinguish within the short duration of every case. Exhausting time and patience like in an intimate chronicle that accepts some formats to become obsolete, others to fall into oblivion. History is for that stream of events, what we happen to recall from a pathetic resemblance.

Pezo von Ellrichshausen, *Finite Format 04*, 729 pieces, watercolour on paper, 21 × 28cm each, 252 × 1701cm overall dimensions, Chicago Architecture Biennial, 2017.

1 Bernard Rudofsky, *Architecture Without Architects: A Short Introduction to Non-Pedigreed Architecture*, New York, Museum of Modern Art, 1964, unpaginated.

2 Nicholas of Cusa, *Nicholas of Cusa on Learned Ignorance. A Translation and Appraisal of De Docta Ignorantia*, Minneapolis, Manning Press, 1981.

3 Plato, *The Republic*, ed. T. Irwin, trans. A. D. Lindsay, London, Everyman, 1992, pp 203–206.

4 Jorge Luis Borges, 'A New Refutation of Time', in *Labyrinths: Selected Stories and Other Writings*, eds. D. A. Yates and J. E. Irby, New York, New Directions Publishing, 2007, pp 217–236; first published as 'Nueva refutación del tiempo' in 1944–46.

5 The complete system is in fact a series of 27 variations (following the basic mathematic operation F = 33). By eliminating all the intermediate stages of the transformation, those with the highest degree of definition are the centralized volume (LLL, MMM or SSS), the flat horizontal planar extension (a grounded building with x, y = L and z = S), the flat vertical planar extension (x or y = L, z = L), the linear horizontal extension (x or y = L and z = S) and the liner vertical extension (x, y = S and Z = L).

6 Increasing the complexity of the rectangular figure, the amount of variations is directly proportional (with four factors: 4F=34=81, five factors: 5F=35=243, and so on). We have painted a complete progression of series, all the way to a rectangular volume with eight factors (which results in 6561 variations). After this large extension, the individual figures start losing their individual character.

1. *The Storyteller - Hatim Tilawon*   2. *The Gardener*   3. *The Fisherman*   4. *The Horticulturist*   5. *The Elevated Public Square*

Between the Borders of Utopia

Towards a Construction of Time

Arinjoy Sen

A place is to be created over an indeterminate period of time, without an end, as a growing, incremental landscape of punctuations and intersections.

The complexity of Kashmir lies in its historical condition. Situated in a valley at the foothills of the Himalayas in the northern region of the Indian subcontinent, Kashmir is divided by a violent border – the 'Line of Control'. An arbitrary line drawn during the negotiated independence of India and Pakistan effectively divided the subcontinent into ideological fragments, shaping the precarious history of a people through conflict and crisis. Such a condition begs us to address the lost identity of a people who have been subjected to a constant territorial tug of war.

Rooted in episodes of cross-pollination during varied political upheavals, Kashmir's complex interwoven identity encapsulates its fragmented culture, architecture, politics and religious affiliations. Between death and democracy, between the military and the militants, between India and Pakistan: a place once known as 'Paradise on Earth' for its geographical beauty and curated presence is now informed by conflict and precarity.[1] This manifests in streets acting as theatres of violence, and daily life subjected to surveillance, choreography and control. The aim of my project is to investigate the historical complexity of Kashmir as a place, as a means to discover its people. Evolving images weave narrative and productive histories together, proposing possibilities of emancipation and autonomy within and against state control, and towards a new grammar for the city.

Arinjoy Sen, *Productive Insurgence*, Srinagar, Kashmir, 2020. Utilisation of traditional practices towards the facilitation of a circular economy.

Productive insurgence:
Exploring the politics of identity, time and medium

Beyond a strictly built manifestation, *Productive Insurgence* investigates two alternative spaces for architectural inhabitation, namely the Kashmiri carpet and the Mughal painting.[2] Both the carpet and the painting occupy a space and purpose within the reality of the project and outside of it. Within the reality of the project, they serve as evolving artefacts and political documents – towards a common construction of history. Outside the project, they allow for an alternative realisation – towards a complex construction of time.

The image of Kashmir is intrinsically linked to the notion of paradise, the Persian origins of which define a political concept.[3] Paradise represents the idea of an exclusive entity, usually a garden, separated from the harshness of the outside world by the bounds of a wall – a state of exception. The project thus explores the idea of paradise in its interpretation as a walled garden, towards a state of exception as an emancipatory apparatus and a localised circular economy. Such possibilities manifest in the project as a network of productive common(s) that punctuate the urban fabric.

The Persian carpet was introduced into India by the Mughal Dynasty in the fifteenth century CE, but the weavers of Kashmir soon made it their own by incorporating specific motifs – like the peacock (national bird of India) denoting royalty, indigo blue denoting solitude and green having religious significance for Muslims.[4] The carpet – deeply ingrained within the

Arinjoy Sen, *Productive Insurgence*, Srinagar, Kashmir, 2020. The political form of the carpet as a manifesto.

culture and traditions of Kashmir – is instrumentalised as a medium, allowing this exploration to transcend the physical limits of the city. More than a domestic artefact, it provides an important space for representation and political reading. Within its own borders, the carpet provides an apparatus for projecting an idea of paradise, at once interwoven with the present and utilising a historical consciousness. The carpet embodies within its material reality a reading of the craft, resources, production and networks of societal and cultural history drawn from the shifting rootlessness of the Silk Route.[5]

Within the reality of the project, the carpet acts both as an evolving document and a building material, thus facilitating the tradition and economy of carpet weaving. A traditional Kashmiri carpet made of pure wool or silk takes anywhere from eight months to more than a year to weave depending on the number of hand-tied knots per square inch (from 600 up to 9,000). The building – which takes a similar amount of time to construct – and the carpet are therefore in latent dialogue with each other, which contributes to the idea of an evolving manifesto. The notion of scripting a manifesto taps into the traditional process of carpet weaving which starts with a *talim* – a code that is used to transfer a design concept and its colour palette, handed from the designers to the weavers.[6] The projection of a new script or grammar for the city involves the hybrid typologies utilised within the project: productive logistics are generated by an insurgent common(s); socio-political and cultural imaginaries are formed by the community.

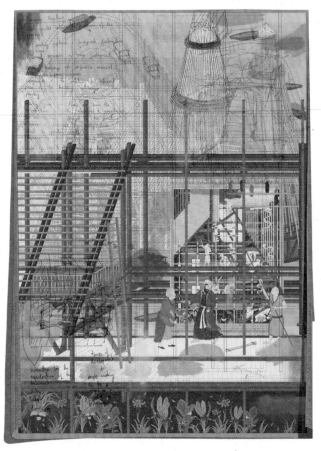

Of carpets and paintings:
Narratives for a new grammar

It is imagined that an alternate manifestation of the project occurs within the apparatus of the Mughal miniature painting, which is deployed here as an ideological plane as well as a manual within the reality of the project. Identity is explored through the painted image, through the projection of a narrative embodied within the infrastructure depicted. The (re)production of architecture then occurs through the production of images.

The role of constructing a narrative is divided between the painted image and the spatial typologies. The built infrastructure of the project employs hybrid spatial typologies as a means to construct a narrative rooted in place, where these spatial typologies are imagined to be characters within a narrative that develops over time, each having a story to tell that is rooted in the struggles of Kashmiris. This is a story told through the local craftsmanship employed in the intricate wooden latticework of *Panjrakari*, the

Left: Arinjoy Sen, *Productive Insurgence*, Srinagar, Kashmir, 2020. An evolving artefact: the painting continuously evolves with the evolution of the building.

Below: Arinjoy Sen, *Productive Insurgence*, Srinagar, Kashmir, 2020. The painting as a manual.

Right: Arinjoy Sen, *Productive Insurgence*, Srinagar, Kashmir, 2020. On the margins of utopia: the painting acts as an ideological plane for the projection of a future that is interwoven with the present.

Himalayan Cedar utilised in traditional timber-framed, stone-infill *Dhajji-Dewari* and *Taq* constructions; the traditional bamboo-weaving of *wagu* and the hand-weaving of carpets. The reinterpretation and subsequent utilisation of these traditional practices within the project allows for the resurgence of the local economy and for the projection of a new grammar for the city.

The space of the painted image attempts to encapsulate this through its depiction of the interrelationship between craftsmanship, labour, knowledge and tradition – both in its image and its material existence. The image evolving – gradually alongside the evolution of the built project – embodies not only a temporal dysfunction through the weaving of alternative realities, but also becomes a medium for the actualisation of the material reality of the project. Therefore, the idea of utopia – either within the conception of the project or its embodiment in the painting – is no unattainable projection; rather it is interwoven with the present, extending infinitely.

1   'Paradise on Earth' is a Mughal epithet attributed to the valley of Kashmir following Emperor Jahangir's proclamation on his visits to Kashmir during his reign between 1605 and 1627.

2   The Mughal painting is a particular style of painting, emerging from Persian miniatures, that developed during the Mughal conquest of India between the sixteenth and eighteenth centuries CE.

3   The word 'paradise', as the very image of a celestial garden, ultimately entered most European languages via the Greek term παραδεισος [paradeisos]. However, its Persian origin is more of a political concept rather than its later (religious) derivations. Etymologically, the definition implies the presence of the 'wall' constructed out of earth; a fortified space surrounded by formidable walls. Hamed Khosravi, 'Paradise', *The City as a Project*, http://thecityasaproject.org/2011/07/paradise/, 2011, (accessed 12 October 2020).

4   Miras Carpet Industries, 'History of Kashmiri Carpets', *Medium*, https://medium.com/@MirasCraftsblr/history-of-kashmiri-carpets-b0ce165f694e, 2020, (accessed 12 October 2020).

5   The Silk Route refers to a network of ancient land trade routes that connected East Asia and Southeast Asia – primarily China – with South Asia, Persia, the Arabian Peninsula and Southern Europe. The route had major contributions to the economic, cultural, political and religious interactions between these regions from the second century BCE to the fourteenth century CE. Amy McKenna, 'Silk Road', *Encyclopaedia Britannica*, https://www.britannica.com/topic/Silk-Road-trade-route, 2020 (accessed 12 October 2020).

6   Prachi Karnawat, 'A Quick Peek into Kashmiri Carpet Weaving', *The Lookout Journal*, https://www.thelookoutjournal.com/issue-7/2017/7/29/kashmiricarpets, 2017 (accessed 12 October 2020).

GROUPWORK + Amin Taha, Clerkenwell Close, 2017. Facade. Photograph, Timothy Soar.

Explore, Restore, Ignore

Etymology and Continuity in Design
Amin Taha

While Karl Marx spent part of his London exile years at the British Library, Gottfried Semper, also fleeing Germany's failed mid-nineteenth century uprisings, prepared his own manifesto at the British Museum. Specifically, within the Assyrian rooms then displaying newly arrived building fragments and friezes with those of a royal throne and stool, crystallising for him the tectonic origins of all applied arts. Semper and Owen Jones, his British contemporary, led a critical reappraisal of the then dominant Neoclassical style. Though neither had issue with reusing past architectural languages, their criticism was directed at use without etymology.[1] Only three, sometimes overlapping, strategies could lead to coherent and meaningful architecture; beauty and wit would follow. First, a learned and faithful working of an established grammar. Second, developing one with contemporary needs, materials and technologies, so that while visually connected to the past it is representative of the present. Third, an immutable tectonic logic of 'joining and binding' are formalised to 'complete' an apparently wholly new architecture yet legible to craftspeople, builders and architects from all eras.[2] For Semper, continuity with the past is not necessarily maintaining the same broader cultural message through the use of an established, perhaps dying, language but is, at least, one of passing on the common tectonic vocabulary to another generation.

Eugène-Emmanuel Viollet-le-Duc and John Ruskin also questioned the contemporary, mostly Neoclassical, wisdom received through Johann Winckelmann.[3] In which, as a proto archaeologist/anthropologist and historian, Winckelmann considered Greek art and architecture to be aesthetically better than all before and after, justifying his argument through their democratic and republican politics. His seemingly empirical survey and conflated political conclusion dovetailed with Enlightenment aspirations and possibly for the first time, in the modern period, defined architecture as an image/ political emblem alone without tectonic reference. A product without a process. In the midst of nineteenth-century industrialisation, a generation of architects such as Semper and Jones began to criticise the 'meaningless imitation and convention' of Neoclassical tropes, piled one atop the other.[4] The deconstruction of antique architecture and furniture led the way for the Viennese Secessionists to at first reduce their work to an expression of material interface, cladding and bolts, metal to stone. Proceeding to layer these 'bones' with, as Semper sought, a new decorative language relevant to their time while maintaining some continuity with the

GROUPWORK + Amin Taha,
Clerkenwell Close, 2017. Facade with
the spire of St James, Clerkenwell.
Photograph, Timothy Soar.

narratives of classical mythology, Egon Schiele, Gustav Klimt and Adolf Loos gradually discarded direct classical symbols for colour and geometric abstractions that became representative of a new generation. Indebted to Semper and Viollet-le-Duc, Otto Wagner, in his inaugural speech as professor of architecture, directed his students to 'the need, ability, means, and achievements of our time', developing a new architecture relevant to the new age.[5] Yet despite these hopeful words, and possibly due to continued conventional teaching methods through drawing boards alone and without physically experimentation with new materials and technologies, that cohort continued to define 'style' as the composition of the drawn image. While adhering to the first two of Semper's strategies, it fell well short of his ambition for a new age to form a wholly new architecture and ornamentation from new tectonics.

Today, steel and concrete frames enabling open plans and detached facades are the default building methodology. The same frame can suspend any style of facade an architect could want. The possibilities are so bewilderingly infinite that architects need no longer follow any tectonic rules, not even those that brought into being the architectural forms being reused and applied.

Within this context sits the Clerkenwell Green Conservation Area, designated as Islington's first, with its uncomfortably malign requests to 'fit-in with' and 'respect' the neighbours. We are not invited for intelligent conversation with the past but 'guided', sometimes 'enforced', by conservation 'officers' to communicate through mimicry. Consequently, a pull towards a common denominator determines new design proposals, leaving Clerkenwell Close with predominantly postwar new-build speculative offices and flats behind half-brick stretcher bond facades on steel or concrete frames, all 'guided' to appear 'Georgictorian'. Alongside pragmatic physical and environmental analysis of a series of internal layout options, our research (explore-restore-ignore) investigated the broader social and historical context. All but vanished abbeys built by Norman invaders; the spot where Wat Tyler was killed, cutting short his rebellion. Oliver Cromwell clearing medieval remains for his own house, which was in turn demolished by the monarchy's restoration. The home of William Morris's printing press, for which Karl Marx wrote and Lenin later used for his Russian language paper. During these consultations and discussions, a young man dressed in the latest fashion yet passionately advocating mimicry of the past was asked by an elderly resident whether he ought to go home and change into tweeds, preferably printed on plastic.

We began with a more literal reference to the first structures on the specific site: half-timber buildings accommodating stables, storage and servants. A self-learning AI structural algorithm was seeded with braced timber frame construction methodology. The task was to lower the overall use of metal while creating a supporting exoskeleton. The result with some occasional human input was one with a strong visual allusion to the past, which pleased the planning case officer but baffled the newly arrived conservation officer. To resolve their argument, the practice thought it best to suggest a further iteration in stone, which the conservation officer perceived as the 'local predominant material', though with 40 years of 'guidance', in fact brick deserved that title. Limestone had built the abbey and served as loadbearing walls and piers for a further thousand years until the early twentieth century. Three fundamental questions arose. Is it structurally sound without the contrivance of internal steel columns, insulation and fire and water proofing? Is it financially viable? What

GROUPWORK + Amin Taha, Clerkenwell Close, 2017. Fallen column with incomplete Ionic carving. Photograph, Timothy Soar.

Designs on History: The Architect as Physical Historian

does twenty-first century stone 'dressing' look like? The same self-learning AI software, but seeded with stone properties, generated the post-and-beam facade. Intriguingly, the uppermost floor counterintuitively increased in size as wind loading demanding a higher mass. The full volume of stone was priced for supply and installation, returning at 25% of the equivalent stone clad steel frame with its layers of water, weather and fireproofing, which the stone exoskeleton would not need. The first two questions answered we turned to 'dressing'. While visiting both the quarry and stonemason's yard to sign-off structural connection details we found a series of 'master blocks' illustrating the three finishes resulting when extracting stone from a quarry, namely sedimentary (natural) cleavage, drilled cleavage and saw cutting. The first two revealed fossilised seashells and ammonites and all three had occasional quartz pockets. When asked why 'natural' finishes provided by installers have none of these, the quarry master shrugged his shoulders, answering that 'no one ever visits a quarry, they just want clean blocks to carve into, even if it means cutting away all that is natural to use as aggregate for roadfill, only to then introduce naturalism with a blowtorch and chisel'. While other cultural traditions, such as those of the Japanese, have for centuries appreciated the aesthetic qualities of found natural finishes, the proposition was challenging for the planning team. Yet after initial scepticism the three types of finish were accepted in the Ruskinian sense, integrating the handcraft and tooling of the quarry master and stonemason with the skills of the structural engineer and architect.[6]

Although the overall composition looks back a millennia, challenging us to build with the same freshly extracted limestone that the Normans introduced to the country, tectonically linking the past with a contemporary language of binding and joining, the expression of structural assembly and 'as found' finishes is deliberately polemical. Clerkenwell Close emphasises the simplicity and ease with which loadbearing stone structures can be erected, no more complex than the first megalithic trabeated structures and without the overt dressed layer of past ornamentation. And what of the day-to-day ground level details and experiences, the tactile elements that Edward R. Ford refers to as 'autonomous': door handles, gates, seats to pause before entering, often without specificity?[7] Scallop shell bolt heads and gate handles are located adjacent to a fallen Ionic capital and fossilised ammonite within a supporting column. Through a colonnade, a pathway

and quiet cloistered garden of pebble mosaics appear as a revealed archaeology. As if the last abbess had been forced to abandon repairs to the older sections as well as a new wing in the up to the minute Ionic style, there are scattered stones carved with medieval dogtooth, ivy capitals, twisting Solomon columns and grotesques. Opposite the site, the eighteenth-century church of St James sits directly on what was once the abbey chapel of St Mary. Camino pilgrims are known to clasp scallop shells, a habit adopted from pagan pilgrims who visited the temple to Venus, the fallen remains of which are under the shrine of St James in the Cathedral at Santiago de Compostela, Spain. Venus was born in the underworld and carried up by the foaming sea on a scallop shell; the Romans having appropriated the Ionic order in her honour from the Greeks. Without resort to nostalgia through architectural pastiche, such scattered, if cryptic, symbols connect to the cultures of the past under our feet and remind us that what we build and evolve can be intrinsically connected by the immutable tectonic elements of architecture.

GROUPWORK + Amin Taha, Clerkenwell Close, 2017. Scallop shell gate bolts and handles. Photograph, Groupwork.

Left: GROUPWORK + Amin Taha, Upper Street, 2017. Corner facade. Photograph, Timothy Soar.

Right: GROUPWORK + Amin Taha, Upper Street, 2017. Disjointed visual narrative of unforgotten awkward histories. Photograph, Timothy Soar.

Where past vocabularies and motifs are directly used, our area of investigation is critical 'reconstruction' through a post-structuralist lens. Three projects – Bayswater Road, Greville Street and Upper Street – span the spectrum between narrative as light fiction, imagining and perhaps caricaturing what their past architects may have completed had they the opportunity, to buildings as political charged protests, challenging the deliberately misremembered narrative of monuments.

Bombed and destroyed during the Second World War, 168 Upper Street marks the northern conclusion of a nineteenth-century parade of shops built to faintly resemble a Palladian palazzo with a central block, symmetrical wings and bookend pavilions. Early consultation illustrated how nostalgia in built form walks hand-in-hand with questions of style and never more so than when all but intact structures such as the remaining portions of the bombed parade are given social status, because of war damage, for instance. The higher the significance the more pressure there is to replicate. Yet, is it physically even possible? Would the same materials and techniques be available, and their assembly meet current building regulations? And what is at the core of this desire? Are these damaged or lost buildings

Left: GROUPWORK + Amin Taha, Upper Street, 2017. Editing the formwork to edit the past. Photograph, Timothy Soar.

GROUPWORK + Amin Taha, Upper Street, 2017. Window.
Photograph, Timothy Soar.

as singularly unique as 'old master paintings' or as
meaningful to national identity as Warsaw's city centre
after Second World War destruction? Succumbing to the
nebulous if not malign conservation 'officer' guidance to
'fit-in' with the neighbours, the aim and result would at
best be the idealisation of a past, at worst a curtailment
of cultural innovation. Such reimagined and rebuilt
structures are inevitably devoid of the unattractive social
realities that formed them and stripped of 'non-period'
historical anomalies that existed before and after the
preferred defined era. These reconstructed buildings
and town centres are in effect monuments, necessarily
simple in narrative and consequently exclusionary and
flawed. 168 Upper Street reconstructs the form and
details of the section destroyed during wartime bombing,
yet deliberately misremembers the idealised period.
Seemingly impenetrable and solid, it is like so many cast
monuments, a monotoned carapace protecting often
empty if not dubious ideals. The clues to a self-critical
narrative are in the misaligned and broken formwork
which when struck, reveals the inherent and permanent
flaws in the material itself and in turn questions any
reconstruction born of unquestioned idealisation.

At Bayswater Road, the desire to live the *belle epoque* dream overlooking Hyde Park and Kensington Garden is represented as a 3mm woven brass veil following the precise details. It appears massive, solid and permanent from a distance, lightweight and ephemeral when close and touched. Suspended from the superstructure, this is Jones and Semper's separated facade as a woven curtain rich in ornament and motifs of past cultures, the contemporary use of which no longer has direct tectonic or symbolic meaning.

Internally, the view is the one from behind the projection screen; the inhabitants' dreams of grandeur by association with the past remaining before their eyes but dominated by the reality outside looking back. Bayswater Road's design is physically a literal extension of the adjacent nineteenth-century 1–9 Inverness Terrace by Mewes Davis Architects built for the Prince of Wales and his lover Lillie Langtry. It reuses the same details at 1:1 but extrapolates the overall urban mansion block model as the original architects may have done given the opportunity. It is in this sense light fiction and light-hearted in its criticism of aspirational development within 'sensitive historic contexts'. Our Greville Street project similarly silhouettes eight demolished buildings including those on Bleeding Heart Yard. The site is most often remembered as Little Dorrit's home in Charles Dickens' novel but takes its name from an inn, where Catholics and Protestants were held before they were hanged, drawn and quartered in neighbouring Smithfield.[8] The eight buildings are resurrected as a ghost of that past, the 3mm veil not touching the ground but reintroducing in 1:1 detail lost shopfronts on Greville Street and a south facing colonnade on Bleeding Heart Yard that expands public space.

Left: GROUPWORK + Amin Taha, Bayswater Road, 2014. *Belle epoque* mansion house completing the urban block.

Below: GROUPWORK + Amin Taha, Bayswater Road, 2014. Interior, Kensington Gardens seen through the veil.

Winckelmann's legacy is hard to shake off. The wish to 'integrate and fit-in' with the group is innate to us, as it is to all social species. Equally entrenched is the mirrored need to bond and defend the group through differentiating the 'other'. This limbic process continues to drive a binary cycle within architecture in the form of 'style wars'. Yet as Rebecca Bigler explains in her research, such prejudices are not innate nor learned though bitter experience but informed by opinion makers, principally parents and teachers.[9] Within architecture we may identify Winckelmann and numerous critics and academics since. More recently, the late Roger Scruton helped central government to consider instituting into law a new era of pattern book design codes to achieve 'beautiful' buildings.[10] It should be noted that, for Scruton, as for Winckelmann, beauty is founded on Greek classical motifs. Semper reminds us that all design is at first formed then refined into cultural symbols through tectonic need. Ruskin and Jones also reinforced the idea that a past architecture must be comprehensively understood before we can work with it and develop from it. Removing the potential for 'meaningless' mimicry introduces opportunities for the lyrical and poetic. The established grammar could be consciously caricatured and used to criticise the concept of restoration, as at Upper Street. Or direct reference and continuity with the past can occur through the choice of materials and associated tectonics as at Clerkenwell Close, where the vanished past is alluded to, and fallen emblems emerge from the ground as resurrected histories on which we stand and build.

GROUPWORK + Amin Taha, Greville Street, 2017. The veil used to repair and increase public space on Bleeding Heart Yard. Render, JORG.

1 Owen Jones, *The Grammar of Ornament*, London, Day and Son, 1856.
2 Gottfried Semper, *Der Stil in der technischen und tektonischen Kunsten* (Style in the Technical and Tectonic Arts: Or, Practical Aesthetics), 1860–62.
3 Johann Winckelmann, *Gedanken über die Nachahmung der griechischen Werke in der Malerei und Bildhauerkunst* (Reflections on the Imitation of Greek Works in Painting and Sculpture), 1756; Johann Winckelmann, *Geschichte der Kunst des Altertums* (History of Ancient Art), 1764.
4 Margaret Olin, 'Self-Representation: Resemblance and Convention in two Nineteenth Century Theories of Architecture and the Decorative Arts', *Zeitschrift für Kunstgeschichte*, vol 49, issue 3, 1986, pp 376–97.
5 Wagner was indebted to Gottfried Semper, *Vorlaufige Bemerkungen uber bemalte Architektur und Plastik bei den Alien* (Preliminary Remarks on Polychrome Architecture and Sculpture in Antiquity) 1834, and Eugène Emmanuel Viollet-le-Duc, *Entretiens sur l'architecture* (Lectures on Architecture), 1863–72. Otto Wagner, 'Inaugural Address to the Academy of Fine Arts', 1894, in *Modern Architecture*, trans. H. F. Mallgrave, Santa Monica, The Getty Center for the History of Art and the Humanities, 1988, p 160; first published as *Moderne Architektur* in 1896.
6 John Ruskin, *The Seven Lamps of Architecture*, New York, Farrar, Straus and Giroux, 1981, p 169; first published in 1849.
7 Edward R. Ford, *The Architectural Detail*, New York, Princeton Architectural Press, 2011, p. 287.
8 Charles Dickens, *Little Dorrit*, London, Bradbury and Evans, 1857.
9 R. S. Bigler, L. C. Jones and D. B. Lobliner, 'Social Categorization and the Formation of Intergroup Attitudes in Children', *Child Development*, vol 68, issue 3, 1997, pp 530–43; R. S. Bigler and L. S. Liben, 'Developmental Intergroup Theory: Explaining and Reducing Children's Social Stereotyping and Prejudice', *Current Directions in Psychological Science*, vol 16, issue 3, 2007, pp 162–66.
10 Ministry of Housing, Communities and Local Government, *Planning for the Future*, 6 August 2020.

**Parallel Geographies,
Choreographies,
Atmospheres and Other
Forms of Monument**

Sumayya Vally

Searching for forms and histories in the architectures of diaspora, migration and the overlooked, perhaps we may find possibilities for forms of representation alongside themes of hybridity. Evolving expressions of identity – the virtual, the embodied, the performed, the atmospheric, the wayward and the supernatural – dance allegorically alongside each other. That which is fluid, shifting, undefined, continuously redefining, evolving, mutating offers other forms of archive and other modes of architecture.

Histories are always present, transferred and translated into the present, exerting their effects surreptitiously. Architecture, propositional though it is, is also always retrospective, positioned in a continuum of thought and politics. We could define architecture as a collective dream; condensing, sorting, remembering, editing and forgetting our history. As a physical condensation of thought and politics, architecture is often employed dangerously. But this same power holds the opportunity for reform. In postcolonial worlds, a fundamental inquiry into the precepts of architectural design and shared histories has the potential to relocate and recontextualise – to work through, and to imagine beyond – our histories. In order to address them, it may be necessary to recompose, remember and reify our histories, precisely in order to disarm them.

Counterspace was founded in 2015 in Johannesburg, against the backdrop of student protests (#FeesMustFall and #RhodesMustFall), the forced removal of several inner-city informal traders (Operation 'Clean-sweep'), the boom related to the re-mining of gold-mine waste and thus rising toxicity in the city, forensic discoveries around land-claim cases and the remnants of previously undocumented Chinese indentured mine workers, the advance of digital advertising and consultations, and amidst a landscape of frustrations related to the apparent inability of the architectural profession and canon to engage with these actual architectures of the city. Challenges, aspirations and desires for Johannesburg and the continent are embodied in each of our projects.

Structures of indexing, archiving, historicising and remembering construct, form and sediment our ways of seeing. In every text, several other texts can be inferred; in every index and library, there are an infinite number of other libraries. Other origins – heard and felt from listening deeply to place – are always possible. There is always architecture waiting to be found in places that are overlooked, or in that which is not apparent or present. Speculative histories, archaeologies and futures. Fragments of histories – in texts, in physical remnants, in ecological consequences – contain a multitude of voices, viewpoints and potential forms. In order to unearth these, and to imagine differently, our lenses for reading, shifting, sorting and crafting archives need to be continuously attentive, vigilant, discursive, varied and multiple.

The earth of a place is an archive of its pasts, presents and futures. It is a physical and material condensation of histories of movement, visions, rituals and politics of place, physically sedimented and printed in its surface. The earth of a place – its soul – is a generative place, a call to work. An inventory of facts, incidents, occurrences and constructs is an ingredient list for speculative histories and futures. In varying configurations, a series of these fragments, read together and crafted across time and geography, contains multiple possibilities for amplifying, sharpening and configuring aspects of our narratives, politics and positions.

Opposite: Counterspace,
Folded Skies,
Johannesburg, 2018–2019.

1. Two billion years ago.
2. Cataclysmic meteor showers change early Earth's chemical composition. A meteor strike drives the compound *Au*, gold, to the surface.
3. Most of the world's gold and diamonds are found in Angola, Botswana, Democratic Republic of Congo, Namibia, Sierra Leone, South Africa and Tanzania.
4. Mathematical and cultural astronomy. An integral part of the continent's story.
5. The myths and legends of Khoi-san folklore.
6. The calendar system of the Dogons of Mali, based on the phases of the moon.
7. The mini megalithic Stonehenge of Nabta Playa in the Sahara.
8. Observations of the skies through ceremonial rock formations, deemed to have been built 2000 years before those at Stonehenge and elsewhere in Europe.
9. The varied spellings of Rhodes, Roades, Rodes and the misread Rhodef. An English surname of great antiquity, first found chiefly in the counties of Yorkshire and Lancashire, it is of pre-seventh-century CE Anglo-Saxon origin.
10. 51.5074° N, 0.1278° W. London.
11. 26.2041° S, 28.0473° E. Johannesburg.
12. Nabta Playa. The reading of celestial phenomena.
13. The rising of the sun at Summer Solstice. The summer rains. Stars are guides across the Sahara.

14. Embodied knowledges carried in the landscape, in cultural values and in seasonal readings of place.
15. Census data of home languages in South Africa, 1996: isiZulu: 24%, isiXhosa: 18%, Afrikaans: 13%, Sepedi: 9%, English: 8%, Setswana: 8%, Sesotho: 8%, Xitsonga: 4%, SiSwati: 3%, Tshivenda: 2%, isiNdebele: 2%.
16. The words for 'private' and 'public' in isiZulu translate to 'intimate' and 'communal'.
17. Languages form and shape world views.
18. Knowledge is passed down through the oral and the aural – through words, stories and rituals.
19. The Anglicising of schools and education in post-Apartheid South Africa.
20. The forms and expressions in Ndebele paintings embody community prayers, self-identifications, values, stories and traditions. In this Counterspace project, *Ndebele Geometries*, 2019, a playscape of three-dimensional forms comes together to create landscapes of cultural expression – a mathematical universe of non-platonic forms tessellate and cohere, unpacked and played out across several locations across South Africa, from supermarket parking lots in rural Limpopo, to rooftops in densely populated Hillbrow, Johannesburg. A stage-set for performance, play and embodied ancestral dialogue.
21. Knowledges are embodied in places and in landscapes.

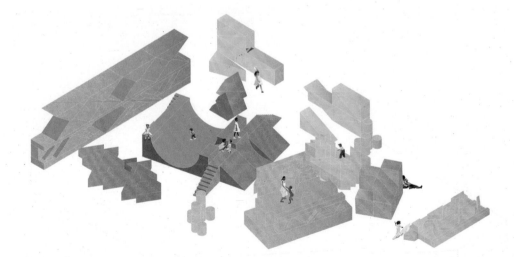

Left: Counterspace,
Ndebele Geometries, 2019.

Designs on History: The Architect as Physical Historian

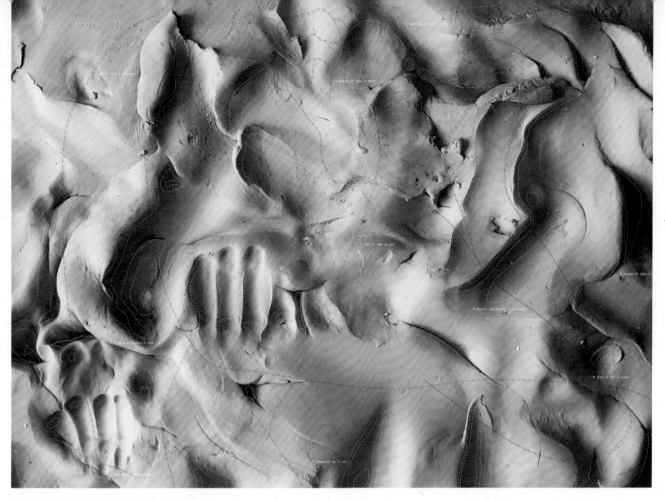

Above: Heidi Lu, *Casablanca: The Port of Homes*, 2019.

22. As language is employed as a form of control, so too are minerals, species and resources employed to deepen the fault lines of control between regions.

23. Cecil Rhodes used his wealth and that of his business partner Alfred Beit to pursue his ambition of carving a British Empire in new territories by obtaining mineral concessions from the most powerful indigenous chiefs.

24. The Middle Ages. Great Britain has large domestic supplies of timber.

25. The famous British oaks.

26. The Malay Peninsula is turned into a plantation economy to meet the needs of industrial Britain.

27. The Industrial Revolution. New materials and designs revolutionise shipbuilding.

28. Bodies and labour are transported across the Atlantic and the Sahara.

29. Heidi Lu, *Casablanca: The Port of Homes*, 2019, tutored by Sumayya Vally, Unit 12, Graduate School of Architecture, University of Johannesburg. This project takes the form of a series of performances and errant surfaces that 'undo' colonial architectural forms in Casablanca. Narrating historical events and intervening in historical architectures, performances, incantations and body rhythms animate, negotiate and arbitrate surfaces – floors, walls and ceilings – in the historic casbahs, hammams and harems. A performance, *How Much Do You Weigh*, invokes the 'weight-passage' in which bodies were weighed to ensure that they were thin and light enough to be carried on slave ships. Lu's body marks and scars the clay floor surface – a homage to rituals of dance and performance of the Gnawa people of Morocco, the present-day descendants of slave-women of the Arab Empire.

30. Silk, textiles, wheat, wood, wool, sugar, tea, tobacco, rubber, palm oil, maize, hemp, gold, guano, mineral fuels, cotton, diamonds.

31. Geographies, soils and species – and their legacies of hybridisation, movement and endangerment – are an evolving archive of our own stories.

32. Fragments of data – hard and soft – trace the shifting of species, geographies and practices. A periodic table of land and sea – excavating and underlining potential histories, potential futures.

Christopher Rojas,
The Zerzura Terrarium, 2019.

33. Christopher Rojas, *The Zerzura Terrarium*, 2019, tutored by Sumayya Vally, Unit 12, Graduate School of Architecture, University of Johannesburg. In response to a brief for a Ministry of Home Affairs situated across the Reunion Island coastline (a French Department on the African continent) in 2018, and as an extension of the brief, a port between Morocco and Spain in 2019, this speculative project proposes a landscape of hybrid species and seasons which narrate histories of movements of peoples across geographies. The terms used to describe species – exotic, endemic, unique, alien – are often the same terms used to classify citizenship. Tapping into various scales – those too big or too small to see, and those moving too fast or too slow to perceive, as well as human and animal scales – the project highlights the connections and links between species' histories and evolutions, empire, extraction, movement, climate shifts and migrations.
34. Territories are bound.

35. In Counterspace's project, *Material Histories: sands, soils, recipes and other archives*, a project for the Istanbul Biennial 2020, a set of recipes is drawn – underlining their cultural use and evolution and the relations between regions. For example, the national dish of Egypt – *Kushary* – finds its roots in homesick Indian soldiers of the British Raj in Cairo, who carried lentils in their pockets and made the Indian dish – *Kitchary* – with several local ingredients. Politics, ecologies and rituals find form in these ingredient lists and communal cooking rituals. Each recipe connects to several others – and the methods of folding the newsprints they are printed on reveal different relations between regions, scales and species. In the project, a series of folding architectures is mapped and designed. In different configurations, and revealing different archival intimacies and relations, these low-tech folding architectures are installed as items of everyday public use – an endless surface unfurls on the market floor as a tablecloth for a communal fast break, a shopfront paste-up and food packaging for market stalls – in markets across Cairo and Casablanca as archives of everyday belonging.

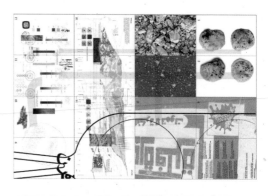

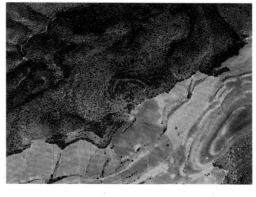

Below: Counterspace, *Material Histories: sands, soils, recipes and other archives*, Istanbul Biennial, 2020.

Above: Counterspace, *Material Histories: sands, soils, recipes and other archives*, Istanbul Biennial, 2020. Section of a *dastarkhwaan*, an eating surface unfurled onto the floor.

aish baladi

عيش بلدي

m'qualli fish tagine

مُقَلِّي

harira

الحريرة

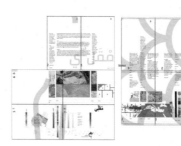
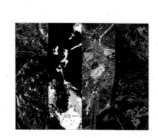

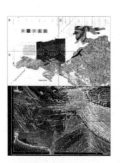
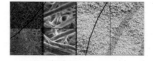

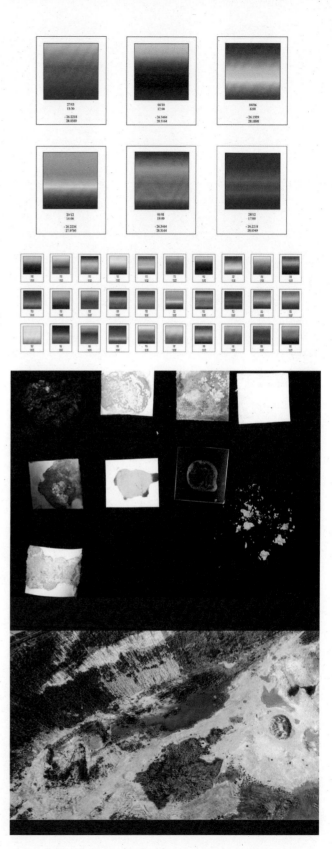

Right top: Counterspace, Colours of Johannesburg skies at different times and different levels of radioactivity, 2020.

Right bottom: Counterspace, Recycled, grafted pigments extracted from a Johannesburg mine dump, with drone photograph, 2015.

36. 1884. John Ruskin's depictions of 'plague clouds' – mass air pollution as a consequence of the Industrial Revolution across Europe.[1]

37. 1886. Gold is 'discovered' in Johannesburg.

38. A city is formed.

39. A connection to deep time is unearthed, as gold mineral, shifted to the surface in the wake of age-old meteorites, is excavated.

40. The mountains of incandescent mine waste are monumental (but eroding) in areas along the gold-reef forming mass-scale architectures when seen from the air in relation to the built form of the city.

41. 1923. South Africa. The Natives Land Act. The Act relegated non-white races to living areas far from the economic centres and nodes. Architecture, urban planning and landscape features were employed in the separation and segregation of the races. Roads, mine dumps and sewerage treatment plants were used to separate people from each other.

42. Designated living areas for blacks are next to radioactive mine dumps.

43. On windy days, some townships are covered in iridescent yellow dust.

44. Buffer-zones for whites are zoos, parks and trees.

45. Counterspace, *Folded Skies*, Johannesburg, 2018–2019, an installation drawing on Johannesburg's atmospheric conditions. As part of Counterspace's longer-term research project, *Ingesting Architectures: on atmospheric violences*, heavy-metal pigments derived from the toxic run-off of mine dumps are extracted and recycled to clean and recycle the water. These pigments are what constitute our city's dust, and its iridescent skies. In this installation, immersive mirrors – which fold light, ground, sky and context (inner-city and its outskirts, mine centre and mine dump) – are tinted with these recycled pigments to create snapshots of Johannesburg skies at different times of the day. A capture of an intangible and atmospheric quality of the city. The mirrors were installed on Johannesburg mine dumps and at Spier Wine Farm in the Western Cape – drawing together interconnected sites and the underbellies of land, resource and power in South Africa.

Designs on History: The Architect as Physical Historian

46. 'The Rhodes Colossus' – a cartoon by Edward Linley Sambourne, published in Punch after Rhodes announced plans for a telegraph line from Cape Town to Cairo in 1892.[2]
47. The export of Africa's resources to Europe.
48. 1900s. Migration on the rise in Britain; migrants are predominantly from British colonies.
49. Southfields, London, 1926 – Al Fazl mosque completed.
50. Mid-twentieth century. The rebuilding of the postwar London economy.
51. An estimated 492 passengers on the HMT *Empire Windrush* arrive at Tilbury Docks on 22 June 1948.
52. 1950s Britain. Jazz, with its transatlantic hybridity – West African slavery, European military bands and instrumentation, American cultural mixing.[3]
53. 1960 to the late 1990s – R & JJ West Indian Restaurant.
54. The collective publishing house and bookshop, Centerprise,
55. Four Aces Club in Dalston.
56. Spaces for British Caribbean people.
57. 2000s – urban renewal and hostility.
58. Counterspace, *Serpentine Pavilion* 2021, Kensington Gardens, London. The Serpentine Pavilion commission was inspired by forms of gathering and belonging in migrant and peripheral communities in London. As a gesture, it folds London into Hyde Park. Pieces of Brixton, Hoxton, Hackney, Tower Hamlets, Whitechapel and North Kensington are traced and amalgamated to form gathering spaces within the Pavilion. Forms are drawn from places of belonging and cultural production both past and present, bringing into being and making visible an archive of belonging for London. Before the Pavilion opens, these places of embodied and erased archive will be activated through a series of events and fragments of the Pavilion – coming together in processions across the city and culminating at the Pavilion in Hyde Park. A folding of the park into the city and of London into the park.
59. History rising to the surface across places.
60. In October 2010, security guards at Langlaagte mine dump noticed human bones sticking out of the ground at one of the mine dumps on site.
61. 650 unmarked graves were discovered.
62. Most of the remains were believed to be those of adult African males. At least two sets of remains were possibly of Asian (Chinese) origin.
63. Questions have emerged why this cemetery, which was one of the largest in Johannesburg between 1890 and 1920, was completely undocumented.

64. Thousands of Chinese mine workers were brought to work in South African mines after the Anglo-Boer War. Many died and were buried at the mines.

65. Porcelain plates and cups of Chinese indentured labourers.

66. Counterspace, *Epochs of Toxicity*, 2020, a ritual ceremony on a piece of leftover land (a mine dump), Johannesburg. A cascade of wardrobes, songs, marronage, letters, fragments from homes past and present, old photos, fossils, a green Zion star badge, a red poster advertising a Valentine's Special, a Shembe ritual staff, the orange peels and eggshells from a Sunday prayer ceremony.

67. A cigarette that costs R1 above ground, costs R100 below. A loaf of bread and a bottle of whisky are also more than 100 times their above-ground price. Grey men live underground for months illegally. Zama-zama means 'try your luck' in Zulu.

68. 2012. A class action lawsuit for 17,000 miners with lung disease is filed.

69. 2018. Mines pay out $400 million USD in settlements dating back to March 1965, the era of the Gold Rush in South Africa.

70. Gold. Acid Yellow. Ferrous yellow and white. Ferrous red. Nickel blue. Nickel green. Copper blue. Seeping. An urban archaeology.

71. The causes and consequences of climate change unfolding.

72. Once numerous, Malayan tigers are classified as a critically endangered species due to habitat loss from logging.

73. 101 companies listed on the London Stock Exchange – most of them British – have mining operations in 37 sub-Saharan African countries.

74. They collectively control over $1 trillion USD worth of Africa's most valuable resources.

75. Active leftovers, quiet histories, silent sovereignties, gradated empires, 'new' categorisations and carceral atlases of colony.

76. Interruptions that meet evidence and archive-like stories that wander into faraway lands and find new tongues. New voices.

77. New futures.

78. New histories.

The shapes of collective memory persist beyond the built. A monument is a verb.

1 John Ruskin, *The Storm Cloud of the Nineteenth Century*, Orpington, George Allen, 1884.
2 Edward Linley Sambourne, 'The Rhodes Colossus Stretching from Cape Town to Cairo', *Punch, or the London Charivari*, 10 December 1892, pp 266–67.
3 George McKay, 'Trad Jazz in 1950s Britain – protest, pleasure, politics – interviews with some of those involved', http://usir.salford.ac.uk/id/eprint/9306, 2001, (accessed 30 November 2020).

Final Word

Jonathan Hill

Editing a book is like organising a party, selecting a theme and inviting guests who will stimulate the conversation. As a book grows in both expected and unexpected ways, the dialogue between editor and contributors is rewarding as well as educating. What then have I learned from editing this volume?

When I first approached Pezo von Ellrichshausen, they emphasised that history was a distant concern, instead proposing that 'perhaps, our fictional roots are pre-historical' and that they wished to expand on these ideas. As there is no virtue in speaking only to the converted, their response convinced me that they would be thoughtful and challenging contributors to this volume. Appropriately conceived by this duo as conjoined streams of consciousness – one visual, the other textual – their article suggests that certain forms and systems may seem simultaneously ahistorical and historical.

Terunobu Fujimori trained as an architect and soon acquired recognition as an architectural historian. At the start of his first significant design commission, he realised that his extensive knowledge of architectural history was limiting as well as advantageous. Terunobu had to forget thousands of years of history in order to reimagine design, identifying an inspiration for green architecture in the Paleolithic and Neolithic period. When everybody else is looking at familiar times and places, it's always good to look elsewhere as a discovery may be yours alone, and thus more surprising for everyone.

In schools of architecture, construction is usually taught as a subject without a history, and meagrely associated with problem solving alone. Instead, Amin Taha delves deep into construction to exploit its poetic and communicative potential. Weaving history and fiction, his designs offer nuanced reassessments of societal values, creatively questioning what we wish to preserve or change. Adopting the past as a model for a more sustainable future, the cover image of this volume – 15 Clerkenwell Close – is the emblem of *The New Stone Age*.[1]

Equivalent to a visual, spatial and textual diary, the process of design – from one drawing to the next iteration and from one project to another – is an autobiographical 'technology of the self', formulating a design ethos for a studio or an individual.[2] Perry Kulper exemplifies this condition. Seeming complete at first sight, his drawings – and those of his students – are consciously unfinished yet caught in a moment. As we developed our back-and-forth dialogue around his article, Perry continued to draw, developing each image and introducing a new one as his contribution coalesced. To involve others in the creative process, Perry avidly exploits social media, notably so during the numerous lockdowns of the pandemic. A slippery palimpsest of thoughts and forms flipping between meanings, Perry's drawings are analogous to his words. Avoiding resolution, they affirm that 'history is a moving target'.

Identifying parallels with Neolithic settlements in Orkney, Níall McLaughlin and Yeoryia Manolopoulou equate architecture to a collective performance binding a community to a place. The term 'design' derives from the Italian *disegno*, which means drawing and associates drawing a line with drawing forth an idea. They introduce a third term – drawing together – to celebrate the social dimension of the design studio. Their site – an archipelago – is an evocatively apt metaphor for simultaneously individual and collective endeavour.

Preparing the article on Unit 12 confirmed how much I have benefitted from discussions with Elizabeth Dow, Matthew Butcher and our students, who were always the first people to know the themes of my next book, including this one. A design studio works best when the students and tutors are each actively engaged on a project, so that their creative dialogue has immediate, tangible effects, facilitating a community of friends and colleagues that can nourish and sustain the creative lives that precede and follow graduation.

The contemporary relevance of interdisciplinary research, which occurs within, between and across disciplines, indicates that a self-contained, insular profession is but one model of practice and implies that a combination of past and future models may be more rewarding. Conjoining principles and practices of architecture and landscape, Aisling O'Carroll employs historical investigation to simultaneously critique and learn from the nineteenth-century architect Eugène-Emmanuel Viollet-le-Duc, reinvigorating reconstruction as a contemporary design practice. A historical design reference need not necessarily be a building or a text but may also be a drawing mode, such as the unfolded interior, three-dimensional map and landscape panorama reimagined by Aisling.

Investigating the migration and translation of ideas, forms and practices, Arinjoy Sen concludes that a design can be a compound of many times and places, and yet also highly specific to one. Emphasising architecture's role in constructing local identities, he conceives design, construction and use – drawing a building as well as building a drawing – as ongoing tools of historical critique, political resistance and collective reimagination.

Emphasising that the foundation of the Graduate School of Architecture (GSA) at the University of Johannesburg was only possible because of the cultural climate generated by student protests, Lesley Lokko celebrates student work as a means to explore and express architectural and personal identities. A design may need to challenge recent history in order to imagine a new future and a new history, notably so in post-apartheid South Africa.

Sumayya Vally defines a monument as a verb and recalls the etymology of the term, which derives from the Latin *monere*, meaning to remind, advise and warn. In post-apartheid Johannesburg, monuments and practices of the apartheid city remain in public view. Conceiving the 'earth of a place as an archive of its pasts, presents and futures', Counterspace redeploys past monuments as material stimuli for design – such as iridescent yellow skies emanating from mountainous radioactive mine dumps – so that their histories can be recalled, disarmed and transformed.

Recognising the overlaps between literary genres, Malcolm Bradbury notably describes his novel *The History Man*, 1975, as 'a total invention with delusory approximations to historical reality, just as is history itself'.[3] One history may need to be categorically rejected in order to formulate another. Instead, selective appraisal may be fruitful. Alternatively, past ideas, forms, practices and histories can be acknowledged as incomplete and ready to be revived, enriched and expanded in the present. Combining investigation and imagination, the physical historian has a responsibility to the future as well as the past.

1 Curated by Amin Taha + GROUPWORK, Steve Webb and Pierre Bidaud, *The New Stone Age* exhibition was held at the Building Centre, London, in 2020, https://www.buildingcentre.co.uk/whats_on/exhibitions/the-new-stone-age-2020-02-27 (accessed 19 April 2021).
2 Michel Foucault, 'On the Genealogy of Ethics: An Overview of Work in Progress' in *The Foucault Reader*, ed. P. Rabinow, London, Penguin, 1984, p. 369; Michel Foucault, 'Technologies of the Self' in *Technologies of the Self: A Seminar with Michel Foucault*, eds. L. H. Martin, H. Gutman and P. H. Hutton, London, Tavistock, 1988, pp 18–19.
3 Malcolm Bradbury, 'Author's Note', in *The History Man*, London, Secker and Warburg, 1975.

Contributors

Elizabeth Dow studied at Kingston Polytechnic and The Bartlett School of Architecture, UCL. Registering as an architect in 1995, from 1998 she combined practice alongside tutoring Bartlett MArch Unit 12. Since 2015 she has also directed The Bartlett's Architectural & Interdisciplinary Studies BSc programme.

Pezo von Ellrichshausen is an art and architecture studio founded in 2002, in the southern Chilean city of Concepción, by Mauricio Pezo and Sofia von Ellrichshausen. They are Associate Professors of the Practice at AAP Cornell University and have been Visiting Professors at GSD Harvard University and Illinois Institute of Technology. Their work has been distinguished with the Mies Crown Hall Americas Emerge Prize, the Rice Design Alliance Prize, the Iberoamerican Architecture Biennial Award and the Chilean Architecture Biennial Award. Among other venues, their work has been exhibited at the Royal Academy of Arts in London, the Art Institute of Chicago, the Museum of Modern Art in New York, and at the Venice Biennale, where they also were the curators of the Chilean Pavilion in 2008.

Terunobu Fujimori is an architectural historian and architect born in Nagano, Japan, in 1946. Currently the Director of Edo-Tokyo Museum and Emeritus Professor at Tokyo University, he has written numerous books on modern architecture, urban planning and street observation. The Green Roof was awarded the 2019 Japan Art Academy Prize.

Perry Kulper is an architect and Associate Professor of Architecture at the University of Michigan. He previously taught at SCI-Arc for 17 years. His interests include the generative potential of architectural drawing; the spatial opportunities offered by utilising diverse design methods; and broadening the conceptual range by which architecture contributes to our cultural imagination. In 2013 he published *Pamphlet Architecture 34, Fathoming the Unfathomable: Archival Ghosts and Paradoxical Shadows* with Nat Chard.

Lesley Lokko is an architectural academic and the author of 11 best-selling novels. She holds a PhD in Architecture from the University of London (2007). Lesley was the founder and director of the Graduate School of Architecture, University of Johannesburg, South Africa, and subsequently Dean of Architecture at the Spitzer School of Architecture, CCNY. Lesley is the founder and director of the African Futures Institute (AFI) in Accra, Ghana. She is the recipient of the 2020 RIBA Annie Spink Award for Excellence in Architectural Education and the 2021 Ada Louise Huxtable Prize for Contribution to Architecture.

Yeoryia Manolopoulou is an architect, co-founder of the studio AY Architects, and Professor of Architecture and Experimental Practice at The Bartlett School of Architecture, UCL. She is the author of *Architectures of Chance* (2013), and lead editor of the *Bartlett Design Research Folios.* In 2014 she was nominated for the Emerging Woman Architect of the Year award.

Níall McLaughlin is an architect. He was born in Geneva and brought up in Dublin, where he studied architecture at University College Dublin. He is principal of Níall McLaughlin Architects and Professor of Architectural Practice at The Bartlett School of Architecture, UCL.

Aisling M. O'Carroll is currently completing her PhD in Architectural Design at The Bartlett School of Architecture, UCL. Her work addresses the relations between history, narrative, and representation in architecture, landscape, geology, examining critical approaches to reconstruction as design. She is co-founder and co-editor in chief of *The Site Magazine.*

Arinjoy Sen is a MArch student at The Bartlett School of Architecture, UCL, tutored in Unit 12 by Elizabeth Dow and Jonathan Hill. His focus ranges from the politics and aesthetics of architecture/space to the instrumentalisation of spatial agents in socio-cultural and political phenomena. Drawing plays a crucial role in Arinjoy's work, where it becomes an apparatus and alternative space for the exploration and subsequent projection of thought processes and architectural discourse. In 2020 he won first prize in the student category of the RIBA Eye Line drawing competition.

Amin Taha was born in East Berlin to an Iraqi mother and a Sudanese father who, marooned after their respective countries underwent counter revolutions, settled in the UK where Amin studied architecture in Edinburgh before working for Zaha Hadid and setting up an independent studio from which GROUPWORK developed as an employee ownership trust.

Sumayya Vally is the Principal of Counterspace and leads Unit 12 at the Graduate School of Architecture, University of Johannesburg. She is searching for design expressions for hybrid identities and territories. Her work is often forensic, and draws on performance, the supernatural, the wayward and the overlooked as generative places of histories and works.

Recommended Reading

Anderson, Stanford, 'The Fiction of Function', *Assemblage*, no. 2, February 1987, pp 19–31.

Banham, Reyner, 'The History of the Immediate Future', *Journal of the Royal Institute of British Architects*, vol 68, no. 7, May 1961, pp 252–260, 269.

Casey, Edward S., *Remembering: A Phenomenological Study*, Bloomington and Indianapolis, Indiana University Press, 2000. First published in 1987.

Cheng, Irene, Charles L. Davis II, and Mabel O. Wilson, eds, *Race and Modern Architecture: A Critical History from the Enlightenment to the Present*, Pittsburgh PA, University of Pittsburgh Press, 2020.

Colonna, Francesco, *Hypnerotomachia Poliphili: The Strife of Love in a Dream*, trans. J. Godwin, London, Thames & Hudson, 1999. First published in 1499.

Davis, Lennard J., *Factual Fictions: The Origins of the English Novel*, Philadelphia, University of Pennsylvania Press, 1996. First published in 1983.

Edgerton, David, *The Shock of the Old: Technology and Global History Since 1900*, London, Profile, 2008. First published in 2006.

Evans, Robin, *Translations from Drawing to Building and Other Essays*, London, Architectural Association, 1997.

Evelyn, John, *Fumifugium: Or, The Inconveniencie of the Aer, and Smoake of London Dissipated*. London, B. White, 1772. First published in 1661 with a slightly different title.

Forty, Adrian, 'Introduction' in *The Art of Forgetting*, eds. A. Forty and S. Küchler, Oxford and New York, Berg, 1999, pp 1–18.

Foucault, Michel, 'Technologies of the Self' in *Technologies of the Self: A Seminar with Michel Foucault*, eds. L. H. Martin, H. Gutman and P. H. Hutton, London, Tavistock, 1988, pp 16–49.

Glacken, Clarence J.. *Traces on the Rhodian Shore: Nature and Culture in Western Thought from Ancient Times to the End of the Eighteenth Century*, Berkeley, University of California Press, 1967.

Gould, Stephen Jay, *Time's Arrow, Time's Cycle: Myth and Metaphor in the Discovery of Geological Time*, London, Penguin, 1990. First published in 1987.

Gregory, Richard, *Eye and Brain: The Psychology of Seeing*, Oxford, Oxford University Press, 1998. First published in 1966.

Halbwachs, Maurice, *The Collective Memory*, New York, Harper Colophon Books, 1980. First published as La Mémoire Collective in 1950.

Haraway, Donna J., *Staying with the Trouble: Making Kin in the Chthulucene*, Durham NC and London, Duke University Press, 2016.

Hulme, Mike, *Why We Disagree About Climate Change*, Cambridge, Cambridge University Press, 2009.

Isozaki, Arata, *Japan-ness in Architecture*, trans. S. Kohso, ed. D. B. Stewart, Cambridge MA and London, MIT Press, 2006.

Lowenthal, David, *The Past is a Foreign Country*, Cambridge, Cambridge University Press, 1985.

Merchant, Carolyn, *Reinventing Eden: The Fate of Nature in Western Culture*, New York and London, Routledge, 2003.

Mithen, Steven, *After the Ice: A Global Human History, 20,000–5,000 BC*, London, Weidenfeld & Nicolson, 2003.

Morrison, Toni, *Playing in the Dark: Whiteness and the Literary Imagination*. Cambridge MA and London, Harvard University Press, 1992.

Nagel, Alexander, and Christopher S. Wood, *Anachronic Renaissance,* New York, Zone Books, 2010.

Palladio, Andrea, *The Four Books on Architecture*, trans. R. Tavernor and R. Schofield, Cambridge MA and London, MIT Press, 1997. First published as *I Quattro libri dell' architettura* in 1570.

Ricoeur, Paul, 'Objectivity and Subjectivity in History' in *History and Truth*, trans. C. A. Kelbley, Evanston, Northwestern University Press, 1965, pp 21–40.

Rudofsky, Bernard, *Architecture Without Architects: A Short Introduction to Non-Pedigreed Architecture*, New York, Museum of Modern Art, 1964.

Rudwick, Martin J. S., *Bursting the Limits of Time: The Reconstruction of Geohistory in the Age of Revolution*, Chicago and London: University of Chicago Press, 2005.

Ruskin, John, *The Seven Lamps of Architecture*, New York, Farrar, Straus and Giroux, 1981. First published in 1849.

Said, Edward, *Culture and Imperialism*, New York, Vintage Books, 1994. First published in 1993.

Scully, Vincent, *American Architecture and Urbanism*, London, Thames and Hudson, 1969.

Soane, John, 'Crude Hints towards an History of my House in L(incoln's) I(nn) Fields' in *Visions of Ruin: Architectural Fantasies and Designs for Garden Follies*, ed. C. Woodward, London, Sir John Soane's Museum, 1999, pp 53-78. Written in 1812.

Tosh, John, *The Pursuit of History: Aims, Methods and New Directions in the Study of History*, London and New York, Routledge, 2015. First published in 1984.

Trachtenberg, Marvin, *Building in Time: From Giotto to Alberti and Modern Oblivion*, New Haven, Yale University Press, 2010.

Vasari, Giorgio, *The Lives of the Most Excellent Painters, Sculptors, and Architects*, trans. G. C. de Vere, New York, Random House, 2006. First published in 1550.

Venturi, Robert, *Complexity and Contradiction in Architecture,* New York, The Museum of Modern Art, 1966.

Vidler, Anthony, *Histories of the Immediate Present: Inventing Architectural Modernism*, Cambridge MA and London, MIT Press, 2008.

Woolf, Daniel, *A Global History of History*, Cambridge, Cambridge University Press, 2011.

Yates, Frances A., *The Art of Memory*, London and New York, Routledge, 1999. First published in 1966.

Index

Aalto, Alvar 23
Accademia del Disegno, Florence, Italy x
Adu-Agyei, Dickson 44
Aicha Qandicha 49
Akasegawa, Gempei 28
Akita Shoukai, Japan 28
Alberti, Leon Battista x, 38
Anachronic Renaissance (Nagel and Wood) x
Anderson, Stanford xiv
Ando, Tadao 23–25
Anthropocene xviii
apartheid 42, 43, 44
Archigram 23
architectonic art 75–83
architectural greening 28–29
Architecture Between Culture, The Highland
    Council, An (student project) 18, 18–19
Art Nouveau 20–21

Banham, Reyner xiv
Barthes, Roland 33
Bartlett School of Architecture, UCL 2–19,
    56–61
Bauhaus xiv, 20, 21, 22
Bayswater Road, London 96, 97, 97
Behrens, Peter 21–22
Beijing Bunny Pagoda (student project)
    35–37, 35
Bentham, Jeremy 35
Bigler, Rebecca 99
Bjerke, Christine 5, 5
Bleeding Heart Yard, London 97
Boon Yik Chung 12, 12
Borges, Jorge Luis 32, 33, 83
Bosch, Hieronymus 38
Bradbury, Malcolm 113
'Bridge: Examining the methods of the
    visionary architect Ledoux', (Fujimori) 23
Bronze Age 20, 25
Brown, Lancelot 'Capability' xviii
Bruegel, Pieter 38
Burbank, Basilica, Beijing: The Architecture of
    Metanarrative (student project) 38, 39

Canary'ed Yellow: Spontaneous Forms (student
    project) 30–31, 41
Capitalocene xviii
carpets, Kashmiri 86–87
Casablanca: The Port of Homes (student
    project) 50, 51, 51, 103, 103
'Celestial Emporium of Benevolent
    Knowledge' (Borges) 32, 33
Cervantes, Miguel de xi
CHATEAU D'ART (Tange) 22, 22
Cho, Hang-Hyun 34, 35
Chthulucene xviii
Cien House, Concepción, Chile 74
Clerkenwell Close, London 90, 91, 92–93,
    92, 93, 99
climate change xvii–xviii, 3

Colonna, Francesco x
Colvin, Brenda xvii
Complexity and Contradiction in Architecture
    (Venturi) 32
Costa, Lucio 28–29
Coulton, Sam 13, 13
Counterspace 52, 100, 101–110, 102, 106,
    107, 108, 109, 110–111
Crude Hints Towards a History of My House in
    L(incoln's) I(nn) Fields (Soane) xiii
Crutzen, Paul xviii

Dandelion House, Japan 28, 28
De architectura libri decem (Vitruvius) x
De Docta Ignorantia (Nicholas of Cusa) 77
De re aedificatoria (Alberti) x
De Stijl 21, 22
Defoe, Daniel xi
Descartes, René 35
Don Quixote (Cervantes) xi
Duchamp, Marcel 33

Église Notre-Dame du Raincy, France 21
Epochs of Toxicity (Counterspace) 110,
    110–111
Euclid's Windmill (student project) 38, 38
Evans, Robin 68
Evelyn, John xi, xvii
Everyday London Archive of Belonging, An
    (Counterspace) 109

Fagus Factory, Germany 21
Farris, Sydney 38, 39
Ferguson, Michael 38, 38
Ferns, Benjamin 8, 9, 9
Fiction of Function, The (Anderson) xiv
Finite Format (von Ellrichshausen) 82, 83
Fischer, Theodor 21
'Five Points Towards a New Architecture' (Le
    Corbusier) 35
Folded Skies (Counterspace) 100, 107
Forbidden City, Beijing, China 38
Ford, Edward R. 93
Foucault, Michel xi, 33
French Revolution 20
Fumifugium: or The Inconveniencie of the Aer
    and Smoak of London Dissipated (Evelyn) xvii
FX Beauties Club (student project) 5, 5

Gaudi, Antoni 23
geological time xvii, xviii
Gibson, William xv
Giedion, Sigfried xiv
global warming xvii–xviii, 3
Goya, Francisco 77
Graduate School of Architecture (GSA),
    University of Johannesburg 43–53, 52,
    103, 104
Grande Salle of La Vedette, The (O'Carroll)
    68, 68

The Grass Roof, Japan 28, 29
Great Lighthouse of Alexandria, Egypt 35
greening, architectural 28–29
Greville Street, London 97, 98, 99
Gropius, Walter xiv, 21, 22, 23
Group Areas Act, South Africa 44
Gubler, Jacques 65
Guinigi Tower, Lucca, Italy 28
Gulliver's Travels (Swift) xi
Guna House, San Pedro, Chile 78, 79
Gut Renovation of the Great Lighthouse of
    Alexandria, (student project) 33, 35

Hadrian's Villa, Tivoli, Italy xii
Haraway, Donna xviii
Hartwell Paper, The xvii, xviii
Hawes, Clare 10, 10–11
Heidegger, Martin 22
Histoire de l'habitation humaine (Viollet-le-Duc)
    67, 68, 68
Historicism 21–22
History Man, The (Bradbury) 113
Holocene xviii
Horyuji Temple, Japan 23
'House of Mud' 25–27
Hulme, Mike xvii
Humphrey, Christopher 37–38, 37
Hypnerotomachia Poliphili (Colonna) x

I Quattro libri dell' architettura (Palladio) viii, x
Immorality Act, South Africa 44
In the Pink: A New United Nations Headquarters
    (student project) 10, 10–11
Industrial Revolution 20, 29, 103, 107
Ingesting Architectures: on atmospheric
    violences (Counterspace) 107
Institute of Landscape Architects xvii
Inverness Terrace, London 97
Ishiyama, Osamu 23–25, 27
Isozaki, Arata x, 23
Ito, Toyo 23–25

Jencks, Charles xiv
Jinchōkan Moriya Historical Museum, Japan
    23–27, 24
John Evelyn Institute of Arboreal Science
    (student project) 1, 3
Jones, Owen 91, 99

Kao Gong Ji x
Kashmir 84, 85–89, 86, 87, 88, 89
Keay, Laura 17, 17
Keller, Mark 33, 35
Klimt, Gustav 91
Kuma, Kengo 27

La Vedette, Lausanne, Switzerland 62–63,
    64, 65–70
Lasdun, Denys xiv, xvi, xvii
Le Corbusier x, xiv, 21, 22, 23, 25, 29, 32, 35

Le Massif de La Vedette (O'Carroll) 68–70, 70–71
Le vite de' più eccellenti pittori, scultori e architettori (Vasari) x
Ledoux, Claude Nicolas 23
Lekalakala, Kgaugelo 44, 44–45
Lévi-Strauss, Claude 38
Liangi, Ifigeneia 6, 6
Living Dam, The (student project) 7, 7
Locke, John xi
London City Farmhouse (student project) 4, 4
London Physic Gardens: A New Necropolis (student project) 13, 13
Loos, Adolf 25, 35, 91
Lu, Heidi 47, 50, 51, 51, 103, 103

McKeon, Michael xi
Mackintosh, Charles Rennie 23
Majolica House, Vienna, Austria 21
Makhubu, Absalom 44
Malan, D. F. 43
Material Histories: sands, soils, recipes and other archives (Counterspace) 106, 106
Mewes Davis Architects 97
Mies van der Rohe, Ludwig 21, 22–23
Minami, Shinbo 28
Ministry of Education and Health Building, Rio de Janeiro, Brazil 28–29
Mme Sureda and Viollet-le-Duc (Viollet-le-Duc) 66
Mme Sureda, the guide and Viollet-le-Duc (Viollet-le-Duc) 67
Modernism xiii–xiv, 20–23, 25
Moll Flanders (Defoe) xi
Monier, Joseph 21
Mont Blanc 65, 70
Moriya Museum see Jinchōkan Moriya Historical Museum, Japan
Morrison, Toni 47
Mosaic Tile Museum, Japan 29, 29
Mthembu, Gugulethu 46, 47, 47, 48, 49, 49
Mughal miniature painting 88–89
Museum of Modern Art, New York 22

Nagel, Alexander x
Natives Land Act, South Africa 107
Ndebele Geometries (Counterspace) 102, 102
Neoclassical 21, 91, 99
Neolithic period 20
    Jomon period, Japan 23–27
    Orkney 16, 56–61
New English Rural, The (student project) 17, 17
Ngũgĩ, Mũkoma wa 53
Nicholas of Cusa 77
Nida House, Navidad, Chile 80, 81
Niemeyer, Oscar 28–29
Nietzsche, Friedrich 20
(No Vacancy/ Nine Lives of the) Land's End Hotel (student project) 36, 37
Noonan, Tom 1, 3

Origins of Architecture and the 2050 UN Climate Summit, The (student project) 16, 16
Orkney vi–vii, 16, 56–61, 60–61
Ouradou, Maurice 68

Paleolithic period 20, 25
Palladio, Andrea viii, x
Panofsky, Erwin x
Pauluskirche, Ulm, Germany 21
Pavillon Suisse, Paris, France 21, 22
Perret, Auguste 21
Pevsner, Nikolaus xiv
Phoenix Palace, World's Columbian Exposition, Chicago 21
Pioneers of the Modern Movement (Pevsner) xiv
Piranesi, Giovanni Battista xii, xiii
Playing in the Dark: Whiteness and the Literary Imagination (Morrison) 47
Pontifical Academy of Sciences (student project) 8, 9, 9
Port of Sihr, The (student project) 46, 47, 47, 48, 49, 49
Portrait of London, A (student project) 12, 12
Posel, Deborah 43
Primary School for Athens, A (student project) 6, 6
Prins, Gwyn xvii
Productive Insurgence (Sen) 84, 86–89, 86, 87, 88, 89

Raymond, Antonin 21
Rayner, Steve xvii
Reich, Kyle 40, 41
Reinanzaka House, Japan 21
reinforced concrete 21, 22, 25
Renaissance ix, x, xiii, 20, 38
re:Quarry'ed (student project) 37–38, 37
Rhodes, Cecil 103, 109
Richards, Emily 36, 37
Ricoeur, Paul xiv
Rietveld, Gerrit 21
Ring of Brodgar, Orkney 57, 61
Rittel, Horst xvii–xviii
Robinson Crusoe (Defoe) xi
Rogue Ornament (student project) 34, 35
Rojas, Christopher 104, 104–105
Rojo Kansatsu Gakkai (Society for Observing the Streets) 28
Roxana (Defoe) xi
Royal Academy of Arts xiii
Royal Institute of British Architects (RIBA) xiv
Royal Society xi, xvii
Rudofsky, Bernard 77
Ruskin, John xv, 91, 99, 107

Saidi, Finzi 44
Sambourne, Edward Linley 109
Santiago de Compostela, Spain 93
Schiele, Egon 91

Schinkel, Karl Friedrich 23
Schröder House, Utrecht, Netherlands 21
Scruton, Roger 99
Scully, Vincent xiv
Seaweed Roof House, Denmark 25, 26
Semper, Gottfried 91, 99
Serpentine Pavilion (Counterspace) 108, 109
Seven Lamps of Architecture, The (Ruskin) xv
Shikibu, Murasaki xi
Shirai, Seiichi 23
Simpson, Isaac Nanabeyin 18, 18–19
Soane, John xiii
Society for Observing the Streets (Rojo Kansatsu Gakkai) 28
Söderberg, Elin 14, 15, 15
Solo House, Cretas, Spain 76, 77
South African Council for the Architectural Profession (SACAP) 53
Space, Time and Architecture (Giedion) xiv
Saint James, Clerkenwell, London 91, 93
Saint Peter's Basilica, Rome 35, 38
Sternburgh, Kallie 36, 37
Stewart, Catrina 4, 4
Stoermer, Eugene xviii
Stone House, Portugal 25, 25
Sullivan, Louis 7, 7
Sureda, Alexandrine 66
Sutro Baths, San Francisco, California 37
Swift, Jonathan xi
Sylva, or A Discourse of Forest-Trees and the Propagation of Timber xvii

Tale of Genji (Shikibu) xi
Tales of the Vulnerability of African Women in Transit Spaces (student project) 44, 44–45
Tange, Kenzō 22–23, 22
Tayob, Huda 52
Technical Administration Building of Hoechst AG, Germany 21–22
Terracotta Warriors 38
Theory and Design in the First Machine Age (Banham) xiv
Trevor-Roper, Hugh 53
Triptychs, Domes + Still Life(s) (Kulper) 40, 41, 41
Tsubokawa-ke House, Japan 25, 27
Twenty-Five Karats: Authentic Fictions (student project) 36, 37

University College London see Bartlett School of Architecture, UCL
University of East Anglia xvi, xvii
University of Johannesburg 43–53, 52, 103, 104
University of Michigan 32–41
Upper Street, London 94–95, 94–95

Vally, Sumayya 47
van Eyck, Jan 38
Vasari, Giorgio x

Vedute di Roma (Piranesi) xii
Venturi, Robert 32
Vers une architecture (Le Corbusier) 32
Verwoerd, Hendrik 43
Vienna Secession 91
Villa Müller, Prague, Czech Republic 35
Villa Tugendhat, Brno, Czech Republic 22
Viollet-le-Duc, Eugène-Emmanuel 62–63, 64,
    65–70, 66, 67, 68, 91
Vitruvius x

Wagner, Otto 21, 91
Walker, Dominic 16, 16
Walt Disney Studios, Burbank, California 38
Wasmuth Portfolio (Wright) 21
Webber, Melvin xvii–xviii
Wei, Luna 35–37, 35
wicked problems xvii–xviii
Winckelmann, Johann 91, 99
Wood, Christopher S. x
Woodland Parliament, The (student project)
    14, 15, 15
Wright, Frank Lloyd 21, 23

Yamada, Mamoru 22
Yoshizaka, Takamasa 25

Zerzura Terrarium, The (student project) 104,
    104–105
Zhao, Yiran 30–31, 41

Image Credits

Cover Image, 90, 91, 92, 94, 95
Timothy Soar / GROUPWORK
iv, v, vi, vii, 54, 55, 58, 59, 60, 61
Nathan Back-Chamness, Luke Bryant, Eleni
Efstathia Eforakopoulou, Ossama Elkholy,
Grace Fletcher, George Goldsmith, Kaiser
Hud, Hanrui Jiang, Rikard Kahn, Cheuk
Ko, Alkisti Anastasia Mikelatou Tselenti,
Veljko Mladenovic, Iman Mohd Hadzhalie,
Andreas Müllertz, Philip Springall and Harriet
Walton with Yeoryia Manolopoulou and Níall
McLaughlin
viii, xii
RIBA Collections
xvi
Lasdun Archive / RIBA Collections
xx, 1
Tom Noonan
4
Catrina Stewart
5
Christine Bjerke
6
Ifigeneia Liangi
7
Louis Sullivan
8, 9
Benjamin Ferns
10, 11
Clare Hawes
12
Boon Yik Chung
13, 122, 123
Sam Coulton
14, 15
Elin Söderberg
16
Dominic Walker
17
Laura Keay
18, 19
Isaac Nanabeyin Simpson
22, 23, 24, 25, 26, 27, 28, 29
Terunobu Fujimori
30, 31
Yiran Zhao
33
Mark Keller
34
Hang-Hyun Cho
35
Luna Wei
36 top
Emily Richards
36 bottom
Kallie Sternbergh
37
Christopher Humphrey
38
Michael Ferguson

39
Sydney Farris
40, 41
Perry Kulper
44, 45
Kgaugelo Lekalakala
46, 47, 48, 49
Gugu Mthembu
50, 51, 103
Heidi Lu
52, 100, 102, 106, 107, 109, 110, 111
Sumayya Vally (Counterspace)
62, 63, 69, 70, 71
Aisling O'Carroll
64, 66, 67
Ministère de la Culture (France), Médiathèque
de l'architecture et du patrimoine, diffusion
RMN-GP.
72, 73, 74, 76, 77, 78, 79, 80, 81, 82
Pezo von Ellrichshausen
84, 86, 87, 88, 89
Arinjoy Sen
93, 96, 97
GROUPWORK
98, 99
JORG / GROUPWORK
104, 105
Christopher Rojas
108
Iwan Baan / Sumayya Vally (Counterspace)

Sam Coulton, *London Physic Gardens: A New Necropolis*, 2018. Aerial perspective with River Thames. See p 13.